HOW TO PASS GCSE ENGLISH LANGUAGE WITH FLYING COLOURS!

An Essential Guide

Nick Evans

English Language and Mathematics are the two core GCSE subjects that all colleges and employers tend to require, regardless of the nature of the college course or employment the candidate is applying for. Students who don't achieve at least a level 4 (regarded as the minimum for a pass) will frequently be required to re-take the subjects until they achieve this level. This guide is specifically designed to quickly and clearly convey tips and techniques to help students to pass GCSE English Language.

The author is an experienced former teacher, private tutor and examiner. Teaching the tips and techniques included in this guide has enabled over 90% of the author's private students in recent years to achieve a pass level in GCSE English Language.

Introduction

This handy guide gives the reader, in a few clear and easy to read pages, all the tools and techniques needed to pass GCSE English Language the first time. Unlike some longer, more costly books, this reader friendly guide cuts right to the heart of the subject, focusing entirely on the examination requirements and assessment criteria, and equipping the reader with the essential skills and techniques to succeed on both the reading and writing sections of the English Language examination papers.

Unlike virtually all other academic subjects, including English Literature, English Language is predominantly more about learning techniques rather than content; it is this aspect that can make the subject challenging for some students, however once they have mastered the techniques and how to apply them, the subject becomes much less daunting.

It isn't strictly true however, that there isn't at least *some* content to learn; it is essential that students acquire a sound knowledge of rhetorical techniques. A thorough understanding of rhetorical / persuasive techniques, and the effects they have upon readers, will help students to accurately analyse the writing of others and allow them to apply these techniques to their own writing, thereby making it more effective. This important aspect of English will be addressed in detail later in this guide.

The guide is primarily aimed at students taking the AQA English Language examination, as that is the examination board the author has most recent experience of and appears to be far and away the most popular choice for institutions in certain regions, however the author has experience of all the other examination boards; the others being: Wjec-Eduquas, Pearson-Edexcel and OCR.

All examination boards now follow the same assessment criteria, therefore the tips and advice in this guide will be relevant to all students regardless of the examination board they are sitting.

In response to reading the following criteria are assessed by all examination boards:

Information retrieval (also known as comprehension or understanding),

Language analysis,

Structural analysis,

Comparative analysis,

Evaluation.

Each of these assessment criteria will be addressed in this guide.

Students will also be required to respond to two writing tasks, which are predominantly: writing to describe, imagine and entertain, and writing to argue and persuade. In other words, they must produce a piece of fictional writing and a piece of non-fiction.

The guide is divided into four chapters.

The first chapter covers the requirements of the reading parts of Papers One and Two of the English Language GCSE examination. It is predominantly focused on the AQA examination, however the assessment criteria and the tips and techniques suggested will be applicable to the English Language papers of all examination boards.

The second chapter focuses on different types of writing and the skills required to produce successful responses in the different writing areas.

The first one is concerned with analytical writing. In other words, how to respond to the reading tasks. Many students often have difficulty with this type of writing, frequently knowing what they want to say but not how to say it. Hopefully this section will give them more confidence regarding writing analytically.

The next two parts of this section focus on the two writing tasks:

Fictional writing (writing to describe imagine and entertain), and non-fictional writing (writing to argue and persuade).

Chapter three uses sources from various examination boards to illustrate how the techniques referenced and discussed earlier can be applied to texts.

Chapter four gives examples of the author's own responses to examination writing tasks. The responses are subsequently annotated to illustrate the language techniques applied in these writing tasks.

One

How to Answer GCSE Language Papers

Introduction.

This guide is predominantly aimed towards the AQA examination paper, however as all examination boards have similar assessment objectives, it is relevant for the other boards too.

All examination boards have **fiction** and **non-fiction** papers for the reading tasks.

The first thing to do once the examination begins is to read the tasks before reading the source material and to highlight the relevant lines / paragraphs on the source material the task refers to, noting the number of marks each section carries. You will then be able to organise your time in line with the marks allocated to each task and focus immediately on the appropriate section, although be aware that with all examination boards and papers there is very likely to be a whole text task at some point.

Do not respond to **any** source material outside the designated lines / paragraphs as, no matter what you say, you will not be credited for referring to material outside the designated sections of each task.

Ensure you match the time spent on each task to the number of marks it carries. Do not run out of time on the higher value tasks at the end. This may seem obvious, but students do frequently run out of time, most often on the later higher value questions.

All English Language reading examination papers tend to have tasks that increase in value, however it is not practical to respond to the highest value question first, as examinations are specifically designed to be worked through in a certain way. Similarly, it is not feasible to attempt the writing tasks before you have completed the reading tasks, as the two are always connected in some way and you might gain ideas or inspiration from the reading tasks. You should also learn from analysing writers' techniques.

Each question on the examination paper has been specifically designed to test one of the assessment objectives and bear this in mind when responding. Examination boards may structure the questions in different order for each task and tasks may vary slightly, but in effect you will be responding to the following skills areas regardless of the examination board.

Understanding - also known as Information Retrieval or Comprehension.

This tests that you can retrieve information from a text and show that you understand it. You are usually asked simply to list, so you don't have to write in full sentences. It is about **what** the writer is saying not **how** he or she is saying it, so you do not have to comment on or analyse the use of language in this task. As this is the easiest task it usually comes first and carries the fewest number of marks on each paper. You should aim to achieve 100% on this task to give you a solid start. Do not spend more than 5 minutes on it. If it asks you to list four points and you think you can list five or more do so. You won't get any more than the maximum marks allowed for the task, but it will ensure you have covered all possibilities. It may be that they are counting two points as one or that one of your points is simply wrong.

On AQA Paper Two (Non-Fiction) comprehension is also tested by asking whether given statements are true or false. Although this task is also usually relatively simple, take care you read the texts very carefully as it is easy to make mistakes on these fifty-fifty answers, and there will often be some statements that require careful consideration as the correct answers will be inferred rather than clearly stated.

Analysis of Language and Structure.

These may be assessed in the same task or separately, dependent on the examination board, but you will be asked at some point to analyse the writer's use of language and structure. If the information retrieval tasks are about **what** a writer is saying this is about **how** he or she expresses it. As language and structural analyses are higher level skills compared to retrieving information the marks are correspondingly higher.

You will need to analyse language techniques and devices. In other words, **why** has the writer chosen certain language techniques and devices? What are they trying to convey? What effects are they trying to create upon the reader? You must use technical terms accurately here. This will show that you know them and help to make your analysis more precise. Do not waste time explaining what a technical term means - your examiner will know this, instead discuss **why** a writer has used it. Note: throughout the guide technical terms appear in red.

Some techniques to look for and to discuss in your language analysis. (See also the techniques to include in the analytical writing section in chapter two where they are discussed in more detail).

Figurative Language: (Similes and metaphors). Why has the writer used them? What are they trying to show or convey?

Adjectives: Positive or negative.

Verbs and adverbs that show feelings are attitudes.

Nouns: Concrete, abstract.

Pronouns: First, second, third person

Sound effects: Alliteration, assonance, onomatopoeia.

Sentence types: Simple, compound, complex.

Sentence functions: Statement, command, question, exclamation.

Viewpoint: First or third person. If third person, the viewpoint will still usually be from that of one character, although occasionally viewpoints may shift.

Tone: Formal, informal or a mixture. Serious, light hearted, ironic. How does the writer convey the tone?

Lexis (Vocabulary): Standard, non-standard, colloquial, dialect. Simple, complex, monosyllabic, polysyllabic. The use of lexis will help to set the tone.

Punctuation, particularly the use of ellipses might be relevant.

Direct speech.

Humour.

Irony.

Appeal to the reader's senses: Sight, sound, taste, touch, smell.

References and examples.

These examples are not exhaustive and there might be others. On the other hand, they won't all be present either.

Structure is the way the writer has organised a text. It could be the order of events in the whole text or within a paragraph or even within a sentence. Why might one event come before another?

Sentence and paragraph links may be relevant. Is information withheld at any point? If so why, what effect does this have? Does the style change at any point? For example, as the text develops does it become increasingly or decreasingly formal or serious? Is it a linear structure? In other words, do the events follow chronologically, or does it employ flashback techniques? Is there a circular structure with the ending reflecting the opening?

When responding to structure you must not just describe **what** happens, but analyse **why** events happen in the order they do. What effect does the structure of a text have upon the reader? For example, it might help the reader to better understand a character's feelings or behaviour, as we will see in one of the textual examples analysed later.

Comparison.

You will be asked to compare and to contrast two texts. This will usually be between two non-fiction texts and probably between a modern and pre-twentieth century text, dependent on the examination board. A pre-twentieth century text is a feature of the modern English Language examination. The language of pre-twentieth century texts will usually be more formal and the sentence structures frequently longer than modern texts, but the ones chosen by the examination boards will still be easily accessible to modern readers, and any words and phrases the board believe will be unfamiliar to students will be explained in a glossary.

Obviously, you must refer to both texts, although it could be that you refer to one more than the other. However, if you do not refer to both you cannot do this task properly. You might also possibly only compare or contrast if you do not find any differences or similarities; however, it is very likely you will do both. You will probably be asked to compare and to contrast language and structural features or ideas and attitudes in the two texts. Language and structure will be the predominant methods writers use to convey their ideas and attitudes, so are linked, and you will usually be expected to do both. Ensure you read carefully exactly what it asks you to compare and to contrast.

Evaluation.

You will be asked to evaluate one or more texts. This means you must give your opinions about it. Analyse **why** you feel it is successful or not. You will be asked to evaluate **how** a writer presents characters in a text and interests the reader in the characters and the narrative. In order to do this task you will draw upon many of the devices listed in the earlier language and structure section.

You must also consider how readers might react to a text. When responding to this task do not use words such as 'good' and 'bad'; instead use terms such as 'effective' or 'successful'. Although you can be critical, you must explain clearly and analytically why you feel this way, never just say 'it is boring'. Instead, you might suggest a metaphor or simile isn't effective and explain why you feel this way. For example, it might be too cliched, or alternatively, too obscure. Always support any judgement you make with evidence or reasons. As these are texts by professional writers which are being used in an examination it is probably best to avoid being critical and to focus instead on what you believe to be the successful or effective aspects of the text concerned.

Two

Writing for Different Purposes

Checklist of techniques for writing Analytically (responding to reading).

As this section gives tips and techniques on how to write when responding to reading, it can also be applied to the Literature examination. Many students frequently suggest they know what they want to say, but they are not sure how to express it; hopefully this section will give them some confidence in the important skill of writing analytically.

Although on the reading sections of Language papers and the whole of the English Literature exam students are assessed on what they say rather than how they say it, examiners are often subconsciously influenced by the way a candidate expresses himself or herself. For example, it is quite possible for an experienced examiner to get an idea from a candidate's very first paragraph of the approximate level the whole paper will ultimately achieve. A skilled writer who employs confident and sophisticated expressions, supported by accurate terminology, can often convey as much in one sentence as a less skilled writer does in a paragraph.

It isn't actually that difficult to achieve a pass grade in English Language (or Literature) provided you demonstrate some understanding and some level of analysis towards texts on the reading task (and your writing is competent and coherent on the writing tasks). However, to achieve the higher levels (7 upwards) a consistent sophistication of expression is frequently required in your response to reading, even if this is seldom explicitly acknowledged in the assessment criteria of examination boards.

Use formal language.

One of the main differences between analytical writing and other types of writing is that you must **always** use formal language. When writing to describe / explain / persuade / argue or imagine / entertain you can use informal, colloquial language if appropriate (unless specified otherwise); in analytical writing you must always write formally. Therefore, do not use phrases such as 'ends up', 'taking the micky', 'freaked out', 'guilt trip', or anything similar. Even terms such as 'mum', 'dad' and 'kids' should be avoided.

Use 'such as' rather than' like' as it is better style.

When adding another point to support one you have just made say 'this reinforces' or 'reinforced by' rather 'than backs' up as it is better style.

Do not say, 'I know this because…' It is unsophisticated. Instead say something such as, 'it is apparent' or 'we can see this / that from / when…'

Do not overuse the phrase 'for example'. It is okay to include it a couple of times in each response, but if you use it before every point you make your responses will seem repetitive and mechanistic. Alternatives are: 'this shows' or 'shown by / when', 'this suggests' or 'suggested by / when', 'this implies' or 'implied by', 'this conveys', 'it is apparent', 'we can see this from / when', etcetera.

Structuring your response.

There are essentially two ways of structuring an analysis. The most obvious is to work through the text you are analysing chronologically; exploring the writer's techniques as you come upon them. The second method is to identify language features that are foregrounded. This is where a language feature might stand out immediately in a text as you read it. Experienced readers are quickly able to identify foregrounding devices and explore them in a non-chronological way.

Different techniques may be foregrounded. An obvious method of foregrounding is the use of repetition, however there are many possible ways. For example, there may be a predominance of figurative language (similes and metaphors) or descriptive language generally - adjectives - which may be positive or negative. Alternatively, it may be the verbs which stand out. Are they active or static? Or are the nouns significant (abstract or concrete?). Sentence structures and length, and the type of lexis may be foregrounded to establish tone or level of formality. The text may employ a lot of dialogue, irony or humour. Pronouns may be significant as they may address the reader. These are just a few examples, however there are many ways of foregrounding. Basically each text will be different, and although techniques for analysis can be learnt, the real skill that enables you to access the higher levels is in being able to confidently identify the methods a writer uses to convey meaning in each particular text and analyse why they have been chosen.

It can be seen therefore that the foregrounding approach to structuring your response is largely more sophisticated and, if executed successfully, more likely to gain a higher level. The foregrounding structural method of analysis is largely employed to the textual examples given in Chapter Three of this guide. However, it is also more challenging than the chronological approach, because it is easy to miss important techniques and if it isn't executed well the response may become confusing. Many candidates may therefore prefer to stick to a chronological response, although this can sometimes lead to a less sophisticated, more mechanistic analysis.

Ultimately, you will have to decide what is best for you. If you feel you are capable of identifying quickly and confidently the techniques that are foregrounded in a source, and able to explore them analytically, then adopt this method of structuring your response. However, if you believe this approach is too challenging, use the chronological structure; you are less likely to miss points and if it is executed well it is still possible to access the higher levels.

Correct style for talking about the writer or the reader.

As you are writing formally, when talking about the writer always use the surname, never just their Christian name, so it is always 'Shakespeare' never 'William'. This applies to every author. It is okay to use a Christian and surname (particularly the first time you refer to them), but to save time it is quicker to just use their surname. As alternatives to constantly writing their name you can say: the writer, author, narrator, speaker, poet, playwright. When writing about some poems you can also sometimes say the 'voice / speaker' as it isn't always the poet. When writing about the main character in a novel or play you can also use the term 'the protagonist'.

When writing about yourself or the reader you can say, 'I feel / I think'. Even better is 'we feel / we think'. Do not use the second person pronoun 'you feel / you think'. That is incorrect style. First or third person only. Alternatively, if it's a novel or poem you are writing about you can say 'the reader, or 'we as readers', or 'the audience' if it is a play you are writing about.

Using quotations.

When analysing the writing of others it is vital to use quotations. They are your evidence that supports your points and analysis. Not only does the use of quotations help to make your analysis more focused and precise, it demonstrates you know the text.

In closed book Literature examinations students naturally worry about accurately reproducing quotations, however you will usually not be penalised for getting them slightly wrong as you are credited for what you actually do with them. It is a good idea though to try to learn by heart around half a dozen all-purpose quotations for each literature text you are studying; ones that can be used to make different points. For example, in *Macbeth* Lady Macbeth's famous lines given below are pretty much essential in any response to the play that involves writing about her character. They show her terrifying ruthlessness and lack of maternal feeling, and can demonstrate how her plea to 'unsex me' earlier in the play has been answered. They also inspire Macbeth to decide to murder King Duncan. Essentially, Shakespeare has chosen the most shocking image he could think of to horrify the audience - that of a mercilessly ambitious woman prepared to brutally kill her baby at the time she should have been nurturing and protecting it. It is a relatively lengthy quotation, but worth learning.

'I have given suck, and know
How tender 'tis to love the babe that milks me.
I would, while it was smiling in my face,
Have plucked my nipple from his boneless gums
And dashed the brains out, had I so sworn as you
Have done to this.'

On the Language papers when you have the text in front of you, you will be expected to quote accurately.

Students also sometimes worry about how many quotations to use in a response. It is not possible to give a number, as it is much more important what you do with the quotations you use, rather than how many you use.

You **must** include quotations in every response, however it is sometimes okay to make points without using a direct quotation, so long as it is still supported with other evidence from the text. E.g. by talking about something a character does. **Never make a point without supporting it, as you will not be credited for unsupported assertions.** Do not quote without analysing or talking about the quotation. Always quote for a reason. If you do not know why you are using a quotation do not use it.

You should include short quotations and integrate them into your own writing. Always give the whole sense of a quotation though. Someone reading your response unfamiliar with the text you are discussing should still be able to understand a quotation you have used. If it is a lengthy quotation use ellipses to save time. Start with the first sense meaning, employ ellipses and then conclude with the end of the quotation. Do not write out great reams of quotations. If you have more quotations than you have your own writing, you are going wrong. You also do not need to say 'this quotation suggests…'

Do not refer to it as a quotation. It is not actually a quotation as such, you are the one quoting. Instead, say something such as 'we can see this from' and then give the quotation. Always use quotation marks to show when you are quoting.

Using technical terms.

You should use technical terms where ever relevant as these will make your response more accurate and sophisticated. Do not use terminology for the sake of it, but only for analysis. You do not need to explain what terms such as: alliteration, assonance, onomatopoeia, simile, metaphor, personification, pathetic fallacy, oxymoron, enjambment, caesura, etcetera, are, assume your reader knows them. However, you must explain **why** the writer has used the technique, what effects are they trying to create? For example, do not say, 'The poet uses alliteration' and leave it at that, explain why the technique has been used or what effect it creates upon the reader.

Similarly, as well as literary technical terms, use grammatical terms; if you know a word is a noun, verb, adjective, adverb, pronoun, etcetera describe it as such, rather than just calling it a 'word'. If you are not sure what word class it is then you can refer to it as a word, however by GCSE you should really be able to distinguish word classes easily and accurately. Similarly, if you know what type a sentence is: simple, complex or compound, or what function it performs; statement (declarative), question (interrogative), or command (imperative) say so if it is relevant for your analysis.

Analysing figurative language.

Analysing the use of similes and metaphors is frequently an essential part of your response to reading. As mentioned above do not just say there is a metaphor or simile and leave it at that, you are unlikely to gain any marks for this. Instead, you need to say **why** the writer has chosen that comparison. What are they trying to show, or what effect on the reader are they attempting to achieve? You can also say if and why you think the image is effective or not. This is called evaluation and an essential part of the assessment criteria on both Language and Literature papers, especially to access the higher levels.

For example, a metaphor could be strikingly vivid and original, alternatively, it could be so obscure that you don't understand it, or the writer has to explain it, in which case it probably isn't an effective comparison. It could also be ineffective because it is a cliched, mundane, over used, metaphor / simile. An effective metaphor or simile should make the reader feel, 'Yes I can see that comparison, but I would never have thought of it.' Again, if a particular type of metaphor is employed, such as personification or pathetic fallacy use the precise term as this will make your response more focused.

If you are unsure about how to analyse figurative language the way it usually works is to compare an abstract concept (something you can't see or touch) with something concrete, in order to make it clearer for the reader.

A good example of this technique is in George Orwell's *Animal Farm* when towards the conclusion of Old Major's speech urging the animals to rebellion he says about the rebellion, 'I do not know when that Rebellion will come, it might be in a week or in a hundred years, but I know, as surely as I see this straw beneath my feet, that sooner or later justice will be done.'

His audience of animals aren't very bright and cannot visualise rebellion, but they can see, smell and touch the straw beneath their feet, therefore Major's simile helps them to understand and to visualise the truth of this abstract concept.

Final checklist.

Check to see you have:

Ensured you have used Standard English and adopted a consistent formal style throughout.

Structured your response clearly and made points which follow logically.

Referred to the author and reader / audience properly as advised above.

Included quotations and discussed how they support your analysis.

Used technical terms accurately where necessary.

Analysed the use of figurative language.

Checklist of techniques to use when writing to Entertain (Imaginative / Creative writing).

Vary your vocabulary.

English is a very rich language with many synonyms (a word or phrase that means exactly or nearly the same as another word or phrase) and you should regularly employ them in order to help to make your writing more varied, sophisticated and entertaining. For example, if writing about children you could also use other terms such as: kids, teenagers, adolescents, young people, youngsters, nippers, brats.

Similarly, old people could be referred to as: pensioners, senior citizens, grannies, oldies, wrinklies, coffin dodgers. Of course, not all terms will always be appropriate as some are non-standard and insulting. Whether you use them or not depends on context. Context, such as the purpose and audience of a piece of writing, are extremely important, therefore in the writing tasks examination boards always tell you who your audience will be and the mode of your task for the response (whether it should be a speech, article, letter, diary entry, blog, etcetera). However, whatever the context, much effective modern writing usually employs a mixture of formal and informal language.

Vary your sentence structures.

Use a variety of sentence structures: simple, compound, complex. Subordination (complex sentences) will make your writing more sophisticated and is one of the features examiners look for in their assessment criteria. Using an embedded subordinate clause (a subordinate clause placed inside a main clause and divided by commas, you could remove it and the rest of the sentence still makes sense) will make your writing appear more competent and sophisticated.

Furthermore, sometimes make use of the present participle form of the verb (ing) to begin a sentence. For example, 'Playing outside, I saw …' rather than, 'I was playing outside, and I saw…' This gives variety to your writing and helps to reduce the over use of 'and' or other connectives.

Good writing uses a variety of sentence structures and sentence lengths. It is often effective to begin or end a paragraph with a short, simple sentence, or to follow a short sentence with a longer one or vice versa.

Use a variety of connectives.

Do not rely on 'and', 'so', 'but' and 'then' too much. Use more sophisticated connectives: however, nevertheless, despite, although, consequently, subsequently, moreover, etcetera. This will make your writing appear more sophisticated. Don't use 'also' too much, and preferably not at the beginning of a sentence. 'Furthermore' is a better alternative.

Choose verbs and adjectives that mean something.

This usually means avoiding neutral, or boring ones, such as: 'walked', 'said', 'go', 'went', 'got', 'nice', 'good,' bad', etcetera.

For example, 'John walked into the room' tells us nothing, whereas, 'John crept, sidled, tiptoed, stormed, marched, strode, blazed, etcetera can give us an immediate insight into John's manner or feelings as he enters the room.

Similarly, 'Janet was thin' (neutral) tells us less than 'Janet was slim' (positive) or 'Janet was skinny' (negative).

'The weather was nice' or 'the weather was hot' tell us little. 'The weather was blazing, baking' or 'the weather was as hot as an oven turn to the maximum' is more vivid. 'Jane has gone shopping' is boring and tells us little. 'Jane has immersed herself' or 'thrown herself into shopping' tells us she enjoys shopping without you having to say so. Make your verbs and adjectives work to convey meaning. This will help you to **show rather than tell**, which is a feature of better writing.

Choose words for their sounds.

Like poetry, good prose often has a rhythm that makes it flow and is both easy to read an easy on the ear. One way of achieving this is to choose words for their sounds. Whenever possible try to employ sound devices such as alliteration and assonance as they can make your writing more effective, adding emphasis or simply making it sound better.

Use references to show rather than tell.

You could also use well known images or references to quickly **show rather than tell**. For example, rather than saying, 'I opened the door to be confronted by a huge, ugly man with a square head and scars on his face,' you could say, 'I opened the door to be confronted by the Frankenstein monster.' Most readers would be able to picture the Frankenstein monster, and immediately know what you are talking about. You do have to be careful with such references however, and choose ones you can be sure your readers will be familiar with. If your readers do not know the reference it will not be effective. This is called extra textual knowledge and requires writers to be aware of their audience. For example, even in the sports pages of 'upmarket' newspapers journalists sometimes make cultural, historical or literary references, as they are aware that their readers are likely to be educated and will get the references, however in the sports pages of the 'popular' newspapers writers will not make such allusions, as they are aware that their readership is unlikely to know the references.

I once had a student responding to an examination descriptive writing task, 'Describe the best or worst meal you have ever had.' She wrote, 'the waiter came running in.' This is pretty bland; to make it a little more interesting, I suggested she change it to 'the waiter came sprinting in like Usain Bolt.' The change of verb to the more specific 'sprinting' from the generalised 'running' and the simile comparing the waiter to the Olympic athlete makes the writing more interesting and humorous. As Bolt was at the time Olympic champion, world record holder and the most famous contemporary sprinter, most readers would be aware of him.

Here is another example of a reference I used taken from a response I wrote to the following examination writing task, 'Describe a time in your life when you were scared and how you overcame it.'

'I guess I have always been a bit of a wimp from the day I saw Gordon Hall, the fat lad, in my primary class, stagger into the classroom, his face bloodied and battered as though he had gone six rounds with Muhammad Ali. Rather than being duffed up by the then heavyweight champion of the world, Gordon had actually had an equally painful encounter with the sheet ice on the school playground.'

As I was writing this, I was aware that, although he was once the most famous man in the world, Muhammed Ali, long out of the public eye, would be unfamiliar to most modern students, therefore I integrated an explanation of who he was. This is one method of explaining a reference, although should not be used too often as it can negate the reference. Ironically, three days after I wrote that, Ali died and for several days was back in the news once more.

Use figurative language.

Using similes and metaphors will make your writing more interesting and entertaining and is an extremely important feature of literary writing whether it is fiction or non- fiction.

A reader should be able to immediately understand a good, original metaphor or simile and think, 'I can see the comparison, but I would never have thought of it!'

It is not easy to think of effective, original similes and metaphors when you are writing under timed conditions and you should try to avoid dead ones (cliched ones that have been done to death), as these are lazy and boring. However, it is better to attempt to use at least some form of figurative language in your writing, even if it isn't particularly original, because at least you will be credited for making the attempt. You could always put a little twist on a cliched metaphor or simile to try to make it appear more original. For example, if you are describing something boring, rather than saying, 'it was like watching paint dry', you could say, 'it was as riveting as gazing at paint drying.' The change of verb from the common 'watching' to the more original 'riveting' makes it sound more emphatic, whilst the assonance of 'gazing at paint drying' adds a touch of humour. These small changes make what is essentially a cliched simile sound fresh.

If you are struggling to think of a simile, animals can often be useful comparisons. For example, if you are trying to describe something fast, slow, large or small try to think of animals which could fall into these categories. 'As slow as a snail,' 'as fast as a cheetah.' Even better, again give a little twist on this. For example, 'as slow as an arthritic snail', or 'as fast as a turbo charged cheetah' helps to make the simile slightly more original and humorous.

Use specific examples.

As with non-fiction writing you should be specific and give examples rather be vague or generalised.

For example, if you are writing a story about a girl who does not get on with her father, rather than just saying she does not get on with her father, describe an incident or example or two to **show** this **rather than just tell**. It could be the time he locked her out of the house or took something from her. This makes it much more interesting for your reader. Again, rather than saying something such as, 'I was scared of the old house', describe in detail what it was about the old house that makes you scared, explain your feelings or the effect it has upon your senses. For example, 'As I crept down the endless gloomy hallway, aware of the creak of every floorboard, my heart began to beat a shade faster and I could taste the fear.'

Appeal to your readers' senses.

Good writing uses language to make the reader see (imagery), hear (sound effects, such as alliteration, assonance, onomatopoeia, sibilance) touch, taste or smell.

Withhold information.

This technique helps to create interest and encourage the reader to want to read on. For example, you can use a pronoun such as he, she, they, them or it before you have explained who or what it is referring to in order to withhold information and build suspense. However, you must eventually reveal who or what it refers to or the reader will feel unsatisfied.

Final checklist.

Check to see you have:

Ensured you have varied your vocabulary and not repeated yourself without good reason.

Varied your sentence structures in terms of length and complexity.

Used a variety of connectives.

Employed interesting verbs and adjectives that show mood, feeling, etcetera.

Used similes and metaphors.

Chosen words and constructed sentences for their sounds.

Given extra textual references and specific examples that show rather than tell.

Appealed to your readers' senses.

Withheld information if and where appropriate.

Checklist of language techniques to include when writing to Argue and Persuade.

Rhetorical devices.

As suggested in the introduction rhetorical devices are an essential component of effective persuasive writing and you must make use of them. There follows a list of common ones and the effects they can produce upon readers.

Rhetorical questions to make the audience think and to make them feel involved. Although a rhetorical question does not require an answer the writer or speaker may well go on to answer the question. Rhetorical questions can be an effective way of opening or closing an argumentative or persuasive piece of writing, especially if it is a speech.

Facts and figures / statistics to give authority and conviction and make the audience believe you know what you are talking about.

Personal experience to make the writing more interesting and relatable for the audience. It is effective to begin with a personal example or experience of the topic and then to open it out more generally. Try to balance facts and figures with personal experience. Always start with personal experience first and then widen your argument as this serves to draw the audience in and helps them to relate to it better than if you begin with statistics.

Emotive language to make the audience feel threatened, angry, guilty or sorry for someone else so they might act. Rhetorical devices can overlap. For example, statistics and facts can often be emotive.

The rhetorical techniques given above are pretty much essential in most persuasive writing and you should nearly always try to include them. The following ones are also useful; whilst you don't always need to include all of them, you should always try to use some of them.

Humour to make your writing entertaining and to encourage your audience to want to listen or read on. Everyone likes to laugh. However, remember humour won't always be appropriate as some subjects might be too serious or sad. For example, if you are writing a charity appeal for people or animals who are suffering in some way humour probably wouldn't be suitable.

Triplets, also known as lists of three, power of three, rule of three. This is where you use three words together to make your writing sound more effective or forceful. For example, rather than saying, 'I disagree with you,' you could say, 'I completely, totally and utterly disagree with you.' This does not actually mean much, but it always sounds more effective and forceful and is a useful rhetorical tool, especially in a speech. When you are using a list of three ensure you put the three words in an effective order. For example, listen for the way they sound together (consider alliteration and assonance) or leave the most original or important word until the last, where it will have the most effect.

Repetition to make your writing more memorable and emphatic. One of the assessment criteria is that good writing should be controlled; this means it should be apparent you know what you are doing, and you are consciously using language purposefully. Examiners will be able to work out whether you have used repetition for rhetorical effect, rather than because you can't think of any other expressions, from the overall effectiveness of your writing. Repetition should be clearly employed for a purpose and not because you can't think of synonyms.

Hyperbole (exaggeration) for emphasis.

Figurative language (similes and metaphors) to make the writing interesting, original and entertaining.

Pronouns. Second person pronoun (you) to make the audience feel they are being addressed directly. First person collective (we) to make an audience feel united. Third person (they / them) to set the audience against someone.

Parallel / balanced constructions to make a speech or piece of writing catchy and memorable. This is where nouns and verbs might be repeated with a slight change in the second part and is a technique often favoured by politicians as they are memorable phrases. Sometimes disparagingly referred to in recent times as 'soundbites' they are still a useful rhetorical tool.

E.g. President Kennedy's famous phrase, 'Think not what your country can do for you, think what you can do for your country.' Or Tony Blair's, 'Tough on crime: tough on the causes of crime.' Note the repetition of nouns and verbs, and in the first example the repeated pronoun.

Calls to action asking the audience to take action. E.g. donate money, sign a petition, write a letter, make a phone call, access a website, etcetera. Calls to action will usually have to come towards the end of a persuasive piece and may be an effective way to conclude your writing.

Structuring your writing.

Beginning.

Do not begin with facts and figures or statistics. This will not engage the reader. Also do not start by referring straight away to a statement you might be responding to such as, 'I agree / disagree with this because…'

If you begin this way you will have immediately given too much away. Instead, try to interest your reader or draw them in by using a 'peg' to introduce your argument. This might take the form of a rhetorical question or a reference to personal experience. This is the way professional journalists often structure their newspaper columns.

The body of your argument.

Discuss the points logically using a new paragraph for each argument and counter argument. Aim for three or four points / paragraphs together with an opening and closing paragraph - five or six in all.

Conclusion.

You could end with a call to action to get your audience to take action as already suggested. Alternatively, you could conclude with a rhetorical question leaving your audience thinking. Another technique is to reference your beginning. This is known as a circular structure and is a popular technique. As the persuasive / argumentative task often gives a statement and invites you to write your views on the statement, in your conclusion you could refer back to the statement in the task. An example of this technique is given in chapter four.

Discourse markers.

You should also make use of discourse markers to help to structure your writing. The discourse is the text and markers help to guide readers through it. Many words and phrases can act as discourse markers. The following are some commonly used ones: Firstly, secondly, on the other hand, in contrast, similarly, despite this, to summarise, in conclusion. You must also employ discourse markers in analytical writing.

Anaphoric / cataphoric references.

Anaphoric reference occurs when a word or phrase refers to something mentioned earlier in the discourse. Cataphoric reference occurs when a word or phrase refers to something mentioned later in the discourse.

These can act as discourse markers. For example, 'the point I made earlier' (anaphoric) or 'I will address this point in due course (cataphoric).

Cohesion / Coherence.

Cohesion is how a text hangs together, in other words its structure. Coherence is if it is understandable. If a text isn't cohesive it may well not be coherent. Using discourse markers will help to make your writing cohesive and therefore coherent.

Final checklist.

Check to see you have:

Ensured you have included some of the rhetorical techniques listed above.

Set out the arguments and your response clearly and logically.

Used discourse markers to make your text cohesive.

Considered opposite sides of the argument and answered the points.

Tried to link points.

Ensured you haven't repeated yourself (unless you are doing so for rhetorical effect).

Used two or three concrete examples to support your argument.

Given a clear conclusion summing up your opinion.

Three

Response to Reading

AQA Specimen Paper One (fiction) reading source.

(Note: all examination boards produce at least one specimen paper for teachers and students to use as practice before a new examination goes live. AQA produced three specimen papers prior to the new examinations beginning in 2017).

Fiction

This extract is from the opening of a novel by Daphne du Maurier. Although written in 1936 it is set in the past. In this section a coach and horses, with its passengers, is making its way through Cornwall to Jamaica Inn.

Jamaica Inn.

It was a cold grey day in November. The weather had changed overnight when a backing wind brought a granite sky and a mizzling rain with it, and although it was now only a little after two o'clock in the afternoon the pallor of a winter evening seemed to have closed upon the hills cloaking them in mist. It would be dark by four. The air was clammy cold and for all the tightly closed windows it penetrated the interior of the coach. The leather seats felt damp to the hands and there must have been a small crack in the roof, because now and again little drips of rain fell softly through, smudging the leather and leaving a dark-blue stain like a splodge of ink.

The wind came in gusts, at times shaking the coach as it travelled round the bend of the road and in the exposed places on the high ground it blew with such force that the whole body of the coach trembled and swayed, rocking between the wheels like a drunken man.

The driver, muffled in a greatcoat to his ears, bent almost double in his seat in a faint endeavour to gain shelter from his own shoulders, while the dispirited horses plodded sullenly to his command, too broken by the wind and the rain to feel the whip that now and again cracked above their heads, while it swung between the numb fingers of the driver.

The wheels of the coach creaked and groaned as they sank into the ruts on the road, and sometimes they flung up the soft spattered mud against the windows, where it mingled with a constant driving rain, and whatever view there might have been of the countryside was hopelessly obscured.

The few passengers huddled together for warmth, exclaiming in unison when the coach sank into a heavier rut than usual, and one old fellow, who had kept up a constant complaint ever since he had joined the coach at Truro rose from his seat in a fury; and, fumbling with the window-sash, let the window down with a crash, bringing a shower of rain upon himself and his fellow passengers. He thrust his head out and shouted up to the driver, cursing him in a high petulant voice for a rogue and a murderer; that they would all be dead before they reach Bodmin if he persisted in driving at breakneck speed; they had no breath left in their bodies as it was, and he for one would never travel by coach again.

Whether the driver heard him or not was not certain: it seemed more likely that the stream of reproaches was carried away in the wind, for the old fellow, after waiting a moment, put up the windows again, having thoroughly chilled the interior of the coach, and, settling himself once more in his corner, wrapped his blanket about his knees and muttered in his beard.

His nearest neighbour, a jovial, red-faced woman in a blue cloak, sighed heavily, in sympathy, and, with a wink to anyone who might be looking and a jerk of her head towards the old man she remarked for at least the twentieth time that it was the dirtiest night she ever remembered, and she had known some; that it was proper old weather and no mistaking it for summer this time, and, burrowing into the depths of a large basket, she brought out a great hunk of cake and plunged into it with strong white teeth.

Mary Yellan sat in the opposite corner, where the trickle of rain oozed through the cracks in the roof. Sometimes a cold drip of moisture fell upon her shoulder, which she brushed away with impatient fingers.

She sat with her chin cupped in her hands, her eyes fixed on the window splashed with mud and rain, hoping with a sort of desperate interest that some ray of light would break the heavy blanket of sky, and but a momentary trace of that lost blue heaven that had mantled Helford yesterday shine for an instant as a forerunner of fortune.

The tasks relating to this source and ways to approach them are given below.

1. Information retrieval.

Read again the first part of the Source from lines 1 to 7.

List **four** things from this part of the text about the weather in Cornwall.
(4 marks)

As suggested earlier this is an easy task and you should not spend more than five minutes on it.

As often with this task it is possible to find more than four things. You could list any four of the following: cold grey day, backing wind, granite sky, mizzling rain, mist, clammy cold, drips of rain.

2. Language analysis.

Look in detail at this extract from lines 8 to 18 (paragraphs 2,3 and 4) of the source.

The wind came in gusts at times shaking the coach as it travelled round the bend of the road and in the exposed places on the high ground it blew with such force that the whole body of the coach trembled and swayed, rocking between the wheels like a drunken man.

The driver, muffled in a greatcoat to his ears, bent almost double in his seat in a faint endeavour to gain shelter from his own shoulders, while the dispirited horses plodded sullenly to his command, too broken by the wind and the rain to feel the whip that now and again cracked above their heads, while it swung between the numb fingers of the driver.

The wheels of the coach creaked and groaned as they sank into the ruts on the road, and sometimes they flung up the soft spattered mud against the windows, where it mingled with a constant driving rain, and whatever view there might have been of the countryside was hopelessly obscured.

How does the writer use language here to describe the effects of the weather?
(8 marks)

There are a number of language features in each of the three paragraphs that can be productively analysed.

In the first paragraph of the section the writer's use of verbs is worthy of comment. She employs the present progressive verb 'shaking' to demonstrate the ongoing effect of the weather upon the coach. The phrase 'the whole body of the coach trembled and swayed, rocking between the high wheels like a drunken man' again uses verbs to show how the coach is being buffeted by the wind, 'trembled' also has suggestions of personification to humanise the coach, whilst the simile 'like a drunken man' helps the reader to visualise the erratic motion of the coach, as they would likely be aware of how a drunken man staggers and sways rather than walks in a straight line. Remember to **always** try to comment on the effects of similes and metaphors.

In the next paragraph the writer has carefully chosen an adjective, verb and adverb 'the dispirited horses plodded sullenly' to show the heavy, slow pace of the horses who have had their spirit knocked out of them and are made miserable by the effects of the weather. We are also given a clear image of how the weather is affecting the driver who is 'muffled in a greatcoat to his ears' and 'bent almost double' as he tries vainly to protect himself from the weather.

The final paragraph of the section makes use of sound devices to help the reader hear the effects of the weather upon the coach. The harsh assonance of 'the wheels of the coach creaked and groaned' helps us to hear how the coach is struggling in the conditions, whilst 'groaned' personifies the coach and makes it seem like a person in pain. Contrasting sounds are then employed. The sibilance of 'flung up the soft spattered mud against the windows' allows the reader to hear the effects of the weather as the language enacts the softer sound of the mud splattering against the windows.

3. Structural analysis.

You now need to think about the whole of the source.

The text is from the opening of a novel.

How has the writer structured the text to interest you as a reader?

(8 marks)

One way of tackling the structure question is to first make a brief note of what each paragraph is about.

For example, the first paragraph is about the weather. The next three paragraphs (the ones discussed in the previous task) then focus more closely on the effects of the weather upon the coach, the horses and the driver. The rest of the text (from line 19) then moves inside the coach as each paragraph is devoted to describing three passengers.

Having established an overview of the content of each paragraph the structure can then be analysed in more detail. Remember, it is vital in this task to discuss **why** a text is structured the way it is, rather than merely describe **what** happens.

Unlike some texts which use flashback or a circular structure, the source employs a linear structure. It begins almost like a film with an establishing shot of the coach as it travels through the stormy weather. It might be described as a long focus overview, which then moves in closer in the next three paragraphs to show the effects of the weather on the coach, horses and driver. We then move inside the coach as the passengers are described in some detail. The writer has therefore taken us from a long focus view, through medium focus to close up by the end of the extract. There is also an effective link between the inside and outside of the coach as one of the passengers thrusts his head through the window to shout to the driver.

The text is structured this way as it allows the reader to immediately see the difficult travelling conditions and realise what the passengers are enduring and why the old man behaves the way he does. We then get brief descriptions of each of the passengers to illustrate their characters and create greater interest in them for the reader. Mary Yellan, who would appear to be the most important character in the story, is significantly the last to be introduced.

In the same way as a cinematic analogy could be used to describe the structure of the source, it could also be suggested that it is about a journey and it takes the reader upon a journey from an awareness of the travelling conditions to some understanding of the characters of the travellers - hence the linear structure.

4. Evaluation

Focus this part of your answer on the second part of the source from line 19 to the end.

A student, having read this section of the text, said, "The writer brings the very different characters to life for the reader. It is as if you are inside a coach with them."

To what extent do you agree?
(20 marks)

This task invites the candidate to **evaluate** how successfully the writer has brought to life the passengers inside the coach and created interest for the reader. It requires **evaluation** of language and structure. Tone and viewpoint may also be relevant, although these will be presented by language and structure. Note: this task is worth 20 marks, making it the highest value task on the reading section of Paper One, and the highest value on the reading section of the entire Language paper. You should therefore spend approximately half the allotted time for the paper on this task (25 - 30 minutes) and ensure you produce a detailed and developed response.

Effective writing can convey a lot of information very quickly and a skilful writer of fiction can create a character within a few lines. Daphne du Maurier successfully portrays and contrasts the three passengers inside the coach in a few paragraphs of telling detail.

The first traveller we are introduced to is a miserable old man. Du Maurier clearly depicts his character immediately when we are told he had 'kept up a constant. complaint ever since he had joined the coach at Truro.' We are given the impression that he is someone who enjoys grumbling. His selfishness and lack of consideration for his fellow passengers are twice touched upon as 'he rose from his seat in a fury; and fumbling with the window sash, let the window down with a crash, bringing a shower of rain upon himself and his fellow passengers.' In the next paragraph we are told he had 'thoroughly chilled the interior of the coach', again indicating he has no thought for others. The verb 'fumbling' suggests that he is so angry he has almost lost control of his fingers, whilst the phrase 'with a crash' emphasises the force of the window coming down.

'He thrust his head out and shouted at the driver in a high, petulant voice.' The verb 'thrust' shows the force of the way he puts his head out and emphasises his anger, whilst the adjective 'petulant' is more usually associated with sulky or spoiled children, rather than a mature adult, and effectively sums up his ill-tempered character. At the end of his description we are told he 'wrapped his blanket about his knees and muttered in his beard.' This confirms the impression we first have of him that he enjoys complaining.

The old man is then juxtaposed with the next character, 'a jovial, red-faced woman in a blue cloak.' Immediately, the adjective 'jovial' suggests she is a happier character than the 'petulant' old man, and this is an effective contrast. She 'sighed heavily in sympathy, and with a wink to anyone who might be looking and a jerk of the head towards the old man, she remarked for at least the twentieth time that it was the dirtiest night she ever remembered, and she had known some...' This suggests that, like the old man, she too enjoys the sound of her own voice, however, unlike him, she is a happy character whose chatting is intended to cheer the other passengers up and distract them from the complaining old man. She also attempts to collude with the other passengers to mock him as she winks at them and jerks her head towards him.

In a good piece of writing every detail is there for a purpose and some readers might be unaware of the significance of the woman eating the cake. This is an important small detail which unequivocally establishes her happy, easy going and confident character. Du Maurier has chosen the language carefully here to convey the woman's character. '...burrowing into the depths of a large basket, she brought out a great hunk of cake and plunged into it with strong white teeth.' Rather than a dainty slice of cake it is a 'great hunk', and instead of cutting it up and eating it delicately with a utensil, she 'plunged into it', the forceful verb emphasising how much she is going to enjoy eating this cake. An important contextual factor here is that the story was set at a time when people did not usually eat in public in the same way they frequently do today. Eating mostly took place in private or in inns, rather than on public transport, and most women at the time would not be seen eating in public, and certainly not consuming a 'great hunk of cake.' This telling detail is symbolic of the woman's character; she is going to enjoy this cake in the same way as she evidently enjoys life and she doesn't care what people think of her. The detail of the cake effectively establishes her character.

The third character described provides a further contrast to the two already introduced. Unlike the previous two, Mary Yellan is named, suggesting she is an important character who is going to play a major role in the story. A further contrast is that the other two characters are extremely talkative in their different ways, whereas Mary Yellan remains silent. This could be because she appears younger than the others, so may be shy, however it is more likely because she is deep in thought. The final paragraph describes how 'she sat with her chin cupped in her hands, her eyes fixed on the windows'. It suggests that she associates the weather with her fortune; the previous day it had been much better, and she longs for the good weather to return as it will herald good fortune. We also learn she is impatient to reach her destination as she brushed the moisture away 'with impatient fingers.'

It can be seen from the above how Daphne du Maurier effectively uses telling little details to quickly and vividly portray the three passengers inside the coach. Structurally Mary Yellan is introduced last as she is the most important and, although it is a third person narrative, the viewpoint seems to be hers as she observes and hears the other two passengers speaking.

AQA Specimen Paper Two (non-fiction) reading sources.

(Note: AQA Paper Two has two reading sources as there are comparative tasks.)

Source A - 21st Century non-fiction.

Could you do your child's homework?

The Observer Sunday 15th December 2013

Children appear increasingly weighed down my homework. But how tough can it be? Jay Rayner attempts his son Eddie's maths assignment.

I am staring at a finely printed sheet of paper and trying not to let the bad feelings seep in. This sheet is all my childhood Sunday night feelings of dread come at once. It is humiliation and 'could do better' and 'pay attention now.'

I only have myself to blame. A few months ago over dinner Eddie announced that, in English, they were experimenting with food writing. 'I have to come up with metaphors. Give me a metaphor about this pizza,' he said. 'I don't think I should do your homework for you,' I said. He raised his eyebrows, 'You can't think of one, can you?' This is what happens if you feed and educate your children. They grow up, become clever and remorselessly take the mickey out of you.

He was right I didn't. On the spot I couldn't think of a single food metaphor worth dragging out and slapping on the table. And so the memories of homework came flooding back: of long nights of carefully planned idleness ruined by the imposition of essays and worksheets, of tasks flunked, of a chilly emptiness at the thought of the way my efforts would be received by teachers. The fact is that I was not especially academic. On the results sheet, my grades lined up like a line of Pac-Men doing a conga.

And so, having failed the English homework test, I decide to show a little solidarity. I will have a go at his maths homework just to get a sense of what it's like to be 14- year-old Eddie. Which is why I'm now staring at the sheet of paper. Ah yes, algebra, the merry dance of x and y. Simplify. Wrench things out of brackets. Calculate values. This, I used to be able to do. Or at least I think I used to be able to do this.

Hmmm. Right. Yes. I mean… I stare at the page again, wondering whether I might be able to will a nose bleed to obscure the equations. There are three marks out of a total of 25 available here. Not getting it right would be an early set back.

The next one looks more straightforward. a4 x a3. I'm pretty sure I remember this. Just add the powers together. Which would mean…

There is an 'expand and simplify' question, which refuses to grow or be simple. In his special mocking voice, Eddie tells me just to draw a sad face. I do as I'm told. Better that than a blank. Eddie returns to his room and I press on. Some of them I can manage. I appear to know how to multiply out 3 (5-2x). But with the next one I am firmly back in the weeds. I'm so baffled that, shamelessly, I Google a maths website.

A few days later Eddie receives his marks. He got 20 out of 25, or 80%, a low score for him. Me? I've got 12 out of 25, or less than 50%. Does it need saying that my biggest miscalculation was to take on Eddie over maths? He doesn't labour the point but he's irritatingly good at it. I knock on his bedroom door. He doesn't look up from his computer screen. He's too busy killing things, while talking on Skype to his friend Theo, who is also in the game trying to kill the same things.

Finally he looks up at me from his computer. Who needs teachers to humiliate you when your son can do it so effectively?

Source B 19th Century literary non-fiction.

This source consists of two letters. The first letter is from a young boy called Henry writing to his father. Henry is living far away from home at a boarding school. A boarding school is a school where you go to live as well as study and was a very popular way of educating boys, especially from wealthier families in the 1800's.

Cotherstone
Academy Aug
7, 1822

Dear Father

Our Master has arrived at Cotherstone, but I was sorry to learn he had no Letter for me nor anything else, which made me very unhappy. If you recollect, I promised that I would write you a sly Letter, which I assure you I have not forgot, and now an opportunity has come at last. I hope, my dear Father, you will not let Mr. Smith know anything about it for he would flog me if he knew it. I hope my dear Father, you will write me a Letter as soon as you receive this, but pray don't mention anything about this in yours; only put a X at the bottom, or write to my good friend Mr. Halmer, who is very kind to me and he will give it to me when I go to Church. He lives opposite and I assure you, my dear Father, they are the kindest friends I have in Yorkshire and I know he will not show it to Mr. Smith for the letters I write you are all examined before they leave the School. I am obliged to write what Mr. Smith tells us and the letters you send me are all examined by Mr. Smith before I see them, so I hope, my dear Father, you will mention nothing of this when you write.

It is now two years come October since I left you at Islington, but I hope, my dear Father, you will let me come home at Xmas that we may once more meet again alive - if God permit me to live as long.

Our bread is nearly black, it is made of the worst Barley Meal, and our beds are stuffed with chaff and I assure you we are used more like Bears than Christians. Believe me, my dear Father, I would rather be obliged to work all my life time than remain here another year.

George is quite well but very unhappy.

Your respectful son

Henry

The second letter, written two weeks later, is from the boy's father to a family friend, asking him to investigate the problem. The father has two sons at the school, Henry and George.

> Public Office,
> Worship Street 21st
> August 1822

Sir

Having lately received a letter from my Son Henry who is at Mr. Smith's School close by you, complaining of the Treatment he receives, I am induced to write to you, confidentially, to request you do me the favour to endeavour to see both of them, privately (at your own house it possible) and ascertain whether you think it would be advisable for me to send for them home. I will certainly be guided by what you say; Boys will sometimes complain without cause, and therefore I hope you will excuse the liberty I take in troubling you. Henry speaks very highly of your kind attention.

I do not approve of the System of Education, for they do not appear to have improved. When they left home, they could both spell, and in Henry's Letter I see several words wrong spelt - I also do not like the injunction laid upon them of not being allowed to write to me without the Master's seeing the contents of their letters.

If you should not be able to get a private interview with them in the course of a fortnight, I shall be obliged by your writing to me to say so and I will immediately give notice to Mr. Smith that I intend to have them home at Christmas. I should prefer your seeing George if you can, and hear what he says, as I can rely more on the truth of his story, than Henry's, for I believe Henry's principal object is to get home. We have all a great desire to see him, but particularly to see George, our other son, who is a meek Boy and not so able to endure ill treatment as Henry - George is a great favourite with us all, and so he was with his late dear Mother who is now no more.

You will no doubt see my object in thus troubling you and I hope you will excuse the liberty I take, but as I know you have been very kind to the Boys. I shall esteem it an additional favour by your attention to this, and an answer at your earliest convenience.

I remain Sir, very respectfully

Your obliged honorable servant

William Heritage

The tasks relating to these sources and ways to approach them are given below.

1. Information retrieval.

Read again the first part of source A from lines 1 to 15

Choose **four** statements below which are true. (4 marks)

A   Jay Rayner has good memories of his time in school.

B   Jay Rayner was happy to help his son with his homework.

C   As a boy, Jay Rayner worried about handing in his homework on Monday mornings.

D   Jay Rayner could not think of a food metaphor to help his son.

E   Jay Rayner was very able in school.

F   Jay Rayner did not enjoy doing homework.

G   Jay Rayner look forward to receiving feedback from his teachers.

H   Jay Rayner makes a joke to cover up his own real exam results.

Although this information retrieval task requires the candidate to simply identify four true statements out of eight given, it is slightly more demanding than the information retrieval question on Paper One.

Rather than just listing as on Paper One, the candidate needs to read carefully to judge whether each statement is true or false. Whilst most of the statements can be identified relatively quickly and easily, on some papers there can be one or two which are more difficult to identify immediately; this is because they aren't always straightforward and require the candidate to demonstrate the skill of inference (working out meaning that isn't openly stated). Although this example isn't as demanding as some others that have been set, there are still statements that infer. The task also usually requires the candidate to read a greater amount of text than does the first question on Paper One. Therefore most candidates will probably spend a little longer on this task than they will on the information retrieval question on Paper One. However, you should still try to keep it to no longer than five minutes.

A. **False.** 'And so the memories of homework came flooding back...of tasks flunked, of a chilly emptiness at the thought of the way my efforts would be received by teachers.'

B. **False.** 'I don't think I should do your homework for you.'

C. **True.** 'This sheet is all my childhood Sunday night feelings of dread come at once.' This is the type of statement referred to earlier that requires candidates to demonstrate the skill of inference. I once had a student who simply would not accept this statement was true as the text does not mention Monday morning. He took everything literally and could not understand that as Sunday night precedes Monday morning Jay Rayner worried about handing in his homework on Monday mornings.

D. **True.** 'On the spot I couldn't think of a single food metaphor worth dragging out and slapping on the table.'

E. **False.** 'The fact is that I was not especially academic.'

F. **True.** 'And so the memories of homework come flooding back: of long nights of carefully planned idleness ruined by the imposition of essays...'

G. **False.** 'A chilly emptiness at the thought of the way my efforts would be received by teachers.'

H. **True.** 'On the results sheet, my grades lined up like a line of Pac-man doing a conga. '

2. Comparative summary.

You need to refer to source A and source B for this question.

Use details from both sources. Write a summary of the differences between Eddie and Henry.
          (8 marks)

There are two main, but related, differences between the two boys. Henry is much more respectful to his father than is Eddie. Source A: 'This is what happens if you feed and educate your children. They grow up, become clever and remorselessly take the mickey out of you' and 'In his special mocking voice Eddie tells me just to draw a sad face.' Eddie also doesn't bother to look up from his computer game when his father enters his bedroom, as though he is dismissive of his father. Source B 'My dear Father' and 'your respectful son,

Henry' illustrate Henry's more respectful attitude towards his father.

There are a number of reasons for the different attitudes displayed by the two boys. Firstly, Henry was living at a time when children would be expected to demonstrate greater respect for their parents; related to this is the fact that Henry is attempting to persuade his father to take him out of school, whereas Eddie seems more academically able than his father, therefore treats him as an equal or even an inferior. Another reason for Eddie's less respectful attitude towards his father is linked with the other major difference between the two boys: Eddie is more academic than Henry which appears to give him more confidence. Eddie received 80% in the Maths test, a low score for him. In contrast Henry's spelling is weak.

Eddie lives at home and appears contented (he plays the computer game after successfully completing his school work), whilst Henry is living away at boarding school where he is very unhappy.

3. Language analysis.

You now need to refer only to source B, the letter by Henry written to his father.

How does Henry use language to try to influence his father?

(12 marks)

Note: the language analysis task on this paper carries more marks than the equivalent question on Paper One (12 as opposed to 8), therefore candidates should spend half the time again as long on it.

This is a relatively easy task on this paper as Henry uses easily identifiable rhetorical devices to persuade his father to take him out of school. (Henry is probably unaware he is employing rhetorical techniques).

In some texts there might be one feature that stands out above all others. This is known as foregrounding and it is what a reader first notices about the text. There are different methods of foregrounding, but a common technique could be the use of repetition, and that is what we get here. Throughout the source Henry constantly refers to his father as 'dear Father.' This is a reminder to his father of his respect. Furthermore, he confirms his respect by signing the letter 'Your respectful son, Henry.' If you show respect towards someone they are much more likely to do what you want them to do than if you don't. Henry is evidently aware of this.

Henry's entire letter is emotive with the intention of making his father feel sorry for him and ultimately to feel guilty for Henry's plight. Henry tells his father that not receiving a letter from him made him feel 'very unhappy'. He gives emotive facts about the conditions he suffers at school: his letters are censored, and he would be flogged if the Master knew he had written to his father. He reinforces the information that he is suffering injustice and cruelty with emotive facts about his living conditions, 'our bread is nearly black; it is made of the worst Barley Meal, and our beds are stuffed with chaff.' He says 'we are used more like Bears than Christians', implying they are treated as badly as bears who at one time were cruelly baited for public entertainment.

He reminds his father how long it is since he left home 'It is now two years come October since I left you at Islington'. He hopes he will be allowed home at Xmas 'that we may once more meet again alive - if God permit me to live as long.' The reference to God is significant as it will play on his father's emotions, suggesting that Henry's fate will remain in the hands of God if his father doesn't allow him to leave school, and that his father has the power of God over his life. He says, 'I would be obliged to work all my life time than remain here another year.' This is a powerful, rhetorical feature, as for a boy from Henry's social background to say he would rather work all his life than continue his education suggests how much he hates the school.

He concludes that George, his brother, is 'quite well but very unhappy.' This is persuasive, as it shows that it isn't just Henry who is unhappy at the school. We also discover in the father's letter that George is the favourite son and the father is more likely to believe George rather than Henry. Although you cannot make reference to the father's letter here, it may be that Henry knows his father is more likely to believe George, and this is another reason why he tells his father that his brother is 'very unhappy.'

4. Comparative exploration of attitudes and methods used to convey those attitudes.

For this question you need to refer to the whole of source A together with source B, the father's letter to a family friend.

Compare how the two writers convey their different attitudes to parenting and education. In your answer, you could:

Compare their different attitudes

Compare the **methods** they use to convey their attitudes

Support your ideas with reference to both texts. (16 marks)

Although this task carries four fewer marks (16 as opposed to 20) than question 4 on Paper One, it is as challenging. Like task 2 on Paper Two it requires a comparative response, however it carries twice as many marks (16 compared to 8) as it requires candidates do more. Task 2 is a straightforward summary; in effect a comparative information retrieval task, with no requirement to analyse the use of techniques. However, this task asks candidates to compare **how** the two writers convey their attitudes. So, unlike task 2, it is not just about **what** the writers say but **how** they say it. Note the use of the word **methods** in the second bullet point. This task is not just about the writers' use of language; other aspects, such as structure, viewpoint and tone could also be explored to achieve the higher levels. Use of language will, however, still be the predominant method chosen for analysis, as it is the way tone is created.

The two writers' attitudes and the methods they use to convey those attitudes are extremely different and lend themselves to rewarding and substantial comparison.

The most obvious difference is the contrasting levels of formality, with source A being quite informal whilst source B is extremely formal. Linked to this are the contrasting tones of the two pieces: Source A is light-hearted and self-mocking; Source B is consistently serious.

Before we explore the methods the two writers employ to create the tone and levels of formality, we need to analyse why they are so different.

Pre-twentieth century writing is usually much more formal than most modern writing. There are numerous reasons for this. Firstly, writers and academics adhered to the prescriptivist view of language - that there is a 'right' and 'wrong' way of writing, and it should always be grammatically correct. If the 'correct' rules of grammar were not followed they believed their readers would not take them seriously. Modern writers and linguists tend to take a more descriptivist view of language - context is more influential than 'correct' grammar, and that suiting language to purpose and audience is more important than adhering to consistently grammatically correct language. Indeed, the terms 'correct' and 'incorrect' are not used today, instead standard and non-standard language are the preferred terms. If non-standard or informal language suits the purpose and audience, then it may be used. As suggested elsewhere, effective writing tends to employ a combination of standard and non-standard language.

A second reason for the greater formality of pre-twentieth century texts is because a contemporary readership would not have anywhere near the distractions modern readers have with the infinitely greater number of medias competing for their attention. Modern readers tend to have much shorter attention spans and are less likely to engage with consistently formal or 'long-winded' texts. The influence of the internet and social media has compounded this shorter attention span, as readers engage with far shorter, informal texts and do not necessarily read them in a linear manner. It is still reading, but reading in a totally different way.

An interesting article about the effect of the internet on our reading and on our attention-spans titled *Is Google Making Us Stupid?* by Nicholas Carr can be found here.

https://www.theatlantic.com/magazine/archive/2008/07/is-google-making-us-stupid/306868/

A highly abridged version of this article was used as an OCR English Language non-fiction examination source in 2013.

The third, and perhaps most important, reason for the contrasting levels of formality and different tones of the two articles can be found in their purposes and audiences. It is essential to recognise that many texts have more than one purpose; usually a primary and a secondary purpose. For example, advertising has the primary purpose of persuasion, however before it can persuade it often has to inform. Similarly, both source A and source B have more than one purpose.

Source A is a public text, published in a national newspaper and potentially read by thousands of people. Although the writer does have a serious purpose - are children given too much, too difficult, homework and could parents do it? (his audience will largely be parents of secondary school children) - as with all modern newspaper columnists he is aware that he must entertain his readership if they are to engage with his article and read it to the end, hence his use of personal experience and humour. In contrast, Source B is a personal letter aimed at an audience of one. The purposes of the letter are to seek information and advice about a serious situation, therefore a light-hearted tone is not appropriate in the context.

We will now explore some of the methods the two writers use to convey their attitudes to parenting and education.

The first example of Jay Rayner's light-hearted tone is when he says, 'On the spot I couldn't think of a single food metaphor worth dragging out and slapping on the table.' Ironically, he has used a metaphor here as it isn't possible to slap an abstract concept, such as a metaphor, on the table. Of course the writer is perfectly aware he has in fact used a metaphor, as he has deliberately employed irony to create humour. He continues with further humorous figurative language when he employs the simile 'my grades lined up like a line of Pac-Men doing a conga.' This is much more vivid and humorous than formally stating his grades were inconsistent.

Non fluency features, monosyllabic one-word sentences and ellipsis are used to show his difficulty and hesitancy when trying to answer the Maths question. 'Hmmm. Right. Yes. I mean…' The sentence structures here contrast enormously with the opening of Henry's father's letter in Source B. The first sentence is very long, taking up most of the opening paragraph. Apart from its grammatical complexity it also features quite formal lexis, such as 'induced', 'endeavour' and 'ascertain.' The serious and formal tone is thereby immediately established. The consistent formality of Henry's father's letter contrasts hugely with Jay Rayner's article which includes such colloquial phrases as 'taking the mickey,' whilst the description of algebra as 'the merry dance of x and y' is amusing and suggests the subject is elusive and toying with him

Jay Rayner again employs ellipsis, 'Which would mean…' to show he is having difficulty working out the maths question. Towards the end of his article he uses the rather vague word 'things' twice when referring to his son's computer game. The repetition of this imprecise word (which would usually be discouraged in most writing) is deliberate to indicate the writer is not familiar with his son's activity; it also reflects Eddie's relaxed confidence after humiliating his father over the Maths task.

Henry's father in source B shows respect to his correspondent throughout the letter, 'I hope you will excuse the liberty I take in troubling you,' and 'I hope you will excuse the liberty I take.' He signs the letter 'Your obliged honorable servant.' By employing this respectful tone he hopes Mr Halmer will supply him with the information and advice he seeks. The formal tone of source B is maintained throughout in such phrases as, 'I also do not like the injunction laid upon them…' and 'I shall esteem it an additional favour by your attention to this…' By employing highly formal language Henry's father hopes to convey how seriously he views the situation and how much he would appreciate Mr Halmer's help and advice.

The writers have differing attitudes to parenting and education. Henry's father is concerned that not only are his sons possibly suffering at the school, but they are not making academic progress '…they do not appear to have improved. When they left home, they both could spell and in Henry's Letter I see several words wrong spelt.' This contrasts with Jay Rayner who has no worries regarding his son Eddie's schoolwork. His only concern appears to be that Eddie is capable of humiliating him with regard to the Maths test.

In Henry's father's letter we learn that he is a single parent, the boys' mother having died. As he doesn't have a wife to discuss parenting and education with, he is forced to seek advice from Mr Halmer. In Source A Eddie's mother isn't mentioned and, as Eddie is confident and academically able, Jay Rayner does not need to ask for advice on parenting and education. The two men also appear to have different attitudes towards their sons' academic work, whereas Jay Rayner gets involved by trying to attempt Eddie's homework, it would probably never occur to Henry's father to become involved in the same way.

Further Examples from Examination Sources.

There follows a small selection of further recent examination sources from various examination boards chosen to illustrate some techniques writers use and how to respond to them.

Fiction

Brighton Rock.

The fiction source on Paper One of the second AQA specimen paper is the opening of Graham Greene's novel *Brighton Rock.* The structure of the famous opening sentence is worth discussing to illustrate how a writer chooses sentence structure deliberately for effect.

In his opening sentence to the novel Greene wrote: 'Hale knew, before he had been in Brighton three hours, that they meant to murder him.'

He could have expressed this in two other ways: 'Hale knew they meant to murder him before he had been in Brighton three hours.'

or

'Before he had been in Brighton three hours, Hale knew they meant to murder him.'

Let us examine why Greene chose the structure he did.

In all sentences there will be one or more words that are more important than the others, these will usually either be verbs or nouns. The key word in this sentence is obviously 'murder'. In a sentence the key word should be placed at the end for effect. This is where it will have the most impact on the reader, as it could create shock or surprise and will be what the reader remembers. This is known as an end weighted sentence, and is a popular structural technique.

Alternatively, for variety or emphasis, the key word could be placed at the beginning of a sentence (front weighted). Least effective of all is to place it in the middle of a sentence, where its impact is lost. This therefore rules out the second possibility, where 'murder' appears in the middle.

The word 'murder' does appear towards the end of the third alternative, however, although more effective than the second example, this isn't as effective as the structure Greene chose.

Let us now examine why this is.

Quite simply, he used the embedded subordinate clause technique, where the subordinate clause 'before he had been in Brighton three hours' is embedded within the main clause and enclosed by commas (take it out and the rest of the sentence still makes sense). By embedding it, rather than placing it before the main clause, as in example three, Greene creates a slight, but important, delay before the reader reaches the shock of the word 'murder'. This is ultimately more effective and heightens the impact of the sentence.

You should always endeavour to structure your own sentences carefully for effect by placing key words where they will have the most impact, and utilising the embedded subordinate clause technique to help create surprise or shock. Employing embedded subordinate clauses can also help to create emphasis and gives a more skilful and sophisticated impression to your writing.

Another feature of Greene's sentence as an effective opening of a novel is the number of questions it raises to engage the reader and encourage them to read on to find out the answers. Who? Why? How? and What?

Who are they?

Why do they want to murder him?

How does Hale know?

What is he going to do about it?

The following source is the pre twentieth century text from Paper Two of the second AQA specimen paper (non-fiction).

Question 3 (the language analysis task) on this paper is as follows:

You now need to refer only to Source B Dickens's description of the fair itself from line19 ('Five minutes walking...') to the end.

How does Dickens use language to make you, the reader, feel part of the fair?

(12 marks)

Non-Fiction

Greenwich Fair: Where Dickens let his hair down.

Charles Dickens is writing in 1839 about a fair in London which was a popular annual event he enjoyed.

The road to Greenwich during the whole of Easter Monday is in a state of perpetual bustle and noise. Cabs, hackney-coaches, shay carts, coal wagons, stages, omnibuses, donkey chaises - all crammed with people, roll along with their utmost speed. The dust flies in clouds, ginger-beer corks go off in volleys, the balcony of every public house is crowded with people smoking and drinking, half the private houses are turned into tea shops, fiddles are in great request, every little fruit shop displays its stalls of guilt gingerbread and penny toys; horses won't go on, and wheels will come off. Ladies scream with fright at every fresh concussion and servants, who have got a holiday for the day, make the most their time. Everybody is anxious to get on and be at the fair, or in the park, as soon as possible.

The chief place of resort in the daytime, after the public houses, is the park, in which the principal amusement is to drag young ladies up the steep hill which leads to the Observatory, and then drag them down again at the very top of their speed, greatly to the derangement of their curls and bonnet caps, and much to the edification of lookers on from below. 'Kiss in the Ring' and 'Threading my Grandmother's Needle', too, are sports which receive their full share of patronage.

Five minutes walking brings you to the fair itself; a scene calculated to awaken very different feelings. The entrance is occupied on either side by the vendors of gingerbread and toys; the stalls are gaily lit up, the most attractive goods profusely disposed, and un-bonneted young ladies induce you to purchase half a pound of the real spice nuts, of which the majority of the regular fair-goers carry a pound or two as a present supply tied up in a cotton pocket-handkerchief. Occasionally you pass a deal table, on which are exposed pennyworths of pickled salmon (fennel included), in little white saucers: oysters, with shells as large as cheese-plates and several specimens of a species of snail floating in a somewhat bilious-looking green liquid.

Imagine yourself in an extremely dense crowd, which swings you to and fro, and in and out, and every way but the right one; add to this the screams of women, the shouts of boys, the clanging of gongs, the firing of pistols, the ringing of bells, the bellowings of speaking-trumpets, the squeaking of penny dittos, the noise of a dozen bands, with three drums in each, all playing different tunes at the same time, the hallooing of showmen, and occasional roar from the wild beast shows; and you are in the very centre and heart of the fair.

The immense booth, with the large stage in front, so brightly illuminated with lamps, and pots of burning fat, is 'Richardson's,' where you have a melodrama (with three murders and a ghost), a pantomime, a comic song, an overture and some incidental music, all done in five and twenty minutes.

'Just a-going to begin! Pray come for'erd, come for'erd,' exclaims the man in the countryman's dress for the seventieth time: and people force their way up the steps in crowds. The band suddenly strikes up and the leading tragic actress, and the gentleman who enacts the 'swell' foot it to perfection. 'All in to begin,' shouts the manager, when no more people can be induced to 'come for'erd', and away rush the leading members of the company to do the first piece.

Suggested response

This task has been chosen as this source is an excellent example of a text where the language can be rewardingly analysed.

In Henry's letter to his father in the previous non-fiction specimen paper, Henry foregrounded his respect by constantly repeating the phrase, 'My dear Father'; in this source Dickens foregrounds the second person pronoun 'you'. In the first sentence of the second paragraph of the section chosen for language analysis he addresses the reader directly, 'Imagine yourself in an extremely dense crowd…' Here he appeals directly to the reader's imagination. He goes on to convey how the reader would be moved about by the crowd 'which swings you to and fro, and in and out, and every way but the right one.' The sentence structure effectively conveys the movement of the individual within the crowd. He concludes this paragraph with another address to the reader, 'and you are in the very centre and heart of the fair.' Although centre and heart have similar connotations, there is a subtle difference which is why Dickens has used both terms. 'Centre' is a mathematical term, whereas 'heart' personifies the fair, giving it a human quality. The use of both terms emphasises to the reader that they are very much part of the fair.

In this paragraph Dickens employs an extensive number of verbs associated with sound to help the reader hear the different noises they will encounter at the fair, 'the **screams** of women, the **shouts** of boys, the **clanging** of gongs, the **firing** of pistols, the **ringing** of bells, the **bellowings** of speaking-trumpets, the **squeaking** of penny dittos, the **noise** of a dozen bands, with three drums in each, all playing different tunes at the same time, the **hallooing** of showmen, and occasional **roar** from the wild beast shows..' Note how he never repeats the same verb, thereby emphasising the variety and excitement of the fair. Furthermore, his use of the present progressive form of the verb (ing) suggests the ongoing excitement. Throughout this paragraph, indeed throughout the whole text, Dickens employs lists of noun phrases to quickly show all the activities at the fair. This is a popular technique when a writer wants to convey a lot of descriptive information quickly - Graham Greene employs the same noun phrase listing technique to describe Brighton in the extract from *Brighton Rock* used on Paper One (fiction) of the second AQA specimen paper.

In the paragraph discussed Dickens has appealed to the readers sense of hearing, and also touch with the movement of the crowd, in the previous paragraph (the first for language analysis) he appeals to the visual sense as he describes the variety of foods on offer.

Again he addresses the reader directly by using the second person pronoun. 'Five minutes walking brings **you** to the fair itself...' '...young ladies induce **you** to purchase half a pound of the real spice nuts...' 'Occasionally **you** pass a deal table...'

Dickens employs alliteration and sibilance to emphasise the sickliness of the snails. 'several specimens of a species of snail floating in a somewhat bilious-looking green liquid.' This is much more emphatic and effective rather than just saying 'snails', as it helps the reader to feel how sickly the snails appear.

In the final paragraph Dickens uses direct speech, 'Just a-going to begin!' Pray come for'erd, come for'erd,' exclaims the man in the countryman's dress...' This conveys the immediacy of the events and helps to make the reader feel part of the fair. As with the use of present tense, direct speech is often more vivid and immediate than reported speech, hence Dickens use of it here; the direct speech is much more effective than if he had reported the man's words.

The following fiction source is from AQA Summer 2017 Examination Paper One (fiction). This was the first live paper of the new examination.

Fiction.

This extract is from the beginning of a short story by Katherine Mansfield. It is the early 1900's and Rosabel, a lower-class girl, who works in hat shop, is on her way home.

At the corner of Oxford Circus, Rosabel bought a bunch of violets, and that was practically the reason why she had so little tea - for a scone and a boiled egg and a cup of cocoa are not sufficient after a hard day's work in a hat shop. As she swung onto the step of the bus, grabbed her skirt with one hand and clung to the railing with the other, Rosabel thought she would have sacrificed her soul for a good dinner, something hot and strong and filling.

Rosabel looked out of the windows; the street was blurred and misty, but light striking on the pains turned their dullness to opal and silver and the jewellers' shops seen through this were fairy palaces. Her feet were horribly wet, and she knew the bottom of her skirt was coated with black, greasy mud. There was a sickening smell of warm humanity - it seemed to be oozing out of everybody in the bus - and everybody had the same expression, sitting so still, staring in front of them. Rosabel stirred suddenly and unfastened the top two buttons of her coat...she felt almost stifled. Through her half-closed eyes, the whole row of people on the opposite seat seemed to resolve into one meaningless, staring face.

She began to think of all that had happened during the day. Would she ever forget that awful woman in the grey mackintosh, or the girl who had tried on every hat in the shop and then said she would 'call in tomorrow and decide definitely'? Rosabel could not help smiling; the excuse was worn so thin.

There had been one other girl - a girl with beautiful red hair and white skin and eyes the colour of that green ribbon shot with gold they had got from Paris last week. Rosabel had seen a carriage at the door; a man had come in with her, quite a young man, and so well dressed.

'What is it exactly that I want, Harry?' she had said as Rosabel took the pins out of her hat, untied her veil, and gave her a hand-mirror.

'You must have a black hat,' he had answered, 'a black hat with a feather on it that goes round your neck and ties in a bow under your chin - and a decent sized feather.'

The girl glanced at Rosabel laughingly. 'Have you any hats like that?'

They had been very hard to please; Harry would demand the impossible, and Rosabel was almost in despair. Then she remembered the big, untouched box upstairs.

'One moment Madam,' she had said. 'I think perhaps I can show you something that will please you better.' She had run up, breathlessly, cut the cords, scattered the tissue paper, and yes there was the very hat - rather large, soft, with a great curled feather and a black velvet rose, nothing else. They had been charmed. The girl put it on and then handed it to Rosabel.

'Let me see how it looks on you,' she said.

Rosabel turned to the mirror and placed it on her brown hair, then faced them.

'Oh Harry, isn't it adorable,' the girl cried, 'I must have that!' She smiled again at Rosabel. 'It suits you beautifully.'

A sudden, ridiculous feeling of anger had seized Rosabel. She longed to throw the lovely, perishable thing in the girl's face, and bent over the hat, flushing.

'It's exquisitely finished off inside, Madam,' she said. The girl swept out to her carriage, and left Harry to pay and bring the box with him.

'I shall go straight home and put it on before I come out to lunch with you,' Rosabel heard her say.

1. Information retrieval.

Read again the first part of the source, from lines 1 to 5.

List four things about Rosabel from this part of the source.

(4 marks)

As often with this task it is possible to find more than four things. You could list any four of the following: she is at Oxford Circus, she bought a bunch of violets, she works in a hat shop, she had a scone, boiled egg and cup of cocoa for tea, she swung onto the step of the bus, she longed for a good dinner.

2. Language Analysis.

Look in detail at this extract, from lines 6 to 14 of the source:

Rosabel looked out of the windows; the street was blurred and misty, but light striking on the panes turned their dullness to opal and silver, and the jewellers' shops seen through this were fairy palaces. Her feet were horribly wet, and she knew the bottom of her skirt and petticoat would be coated with black, greasy mud. There was a sickening smell of warm humanity - it seemed to be oozing out of everybody in the bus - and everybody had the same expression, sitting so still, staring in front of them. Rosabel stirred suddenly and unfastened the two top buttons of her coat... she felt almost stifled. Through her half-closed eyes, the whole row of people on the opposite seat seemed to resolve into one meaningless, staring face.

How does the writer use language here to describe Rosabel's bus journey home?

You could include the writer's choice of:

•words and phrases

•language features and techniques

•sentence forms. (8 marks)

Although the source is a third person narrative, the viewpoint is clearly Rosabel's and Katherine Mansfield employs language techniques to convey how Rosabel feels about the bus journey. The most notable device is the use of a metaphor, 'the jeweller's shops were fairy palaces.' This metaphor reflects how Rosabel views the jewellers' shops: they are like a fantasy for her and their magical glamour contrasts with the stuffy, claustrophobic, repulsive reality of her situation inside the bus.

'There was a sickening smell of warm humanity - it seemed to be oozing out of everybody in the bus -' The alliteration emphasises Rosabel's feelings of repulsion, it also dehumanises the passengers on the bus whom Rosabel doesn't view as individuals, whilst the sound of the verb 'oozing' also conveys an unpleasant feeling. The dehumanisation of the passengers is again suggested by, 'everybody had the same expression' and reinforced by the phrase, 'the whole row of people on the opposite seat seemed to resolve into one meaningless, staring face.'

Despite Rosabel's revulsion of her fellow passengers, she is aware that her own appearance is no different to theirs, 'she knew the bottom of her skirt and petticoat would be coated with black, greasy mud.' This awareness that she is the same as the other passengers, despite her aspirations and fantasy about 'fairy palaces', accounts for Rosabel's anger when she thinks of her encounter with the privileged, red-haired customer earlier in the day.

3. Structural analysis.

You now need to think about the whole of the source. This text is from the beginning of a short story. How has the writer structured the text to interest you as a reader? You could write about:

•what the writer focuses your attention on at the beginning of the source

•how and why the writer changes this focus as the source develops

•any other structural features that interest you.
(8 marks)

This source employs a non-linear flashback structure, which is clearly signposted at the beginning of the third paragraph, 'She began to think of all that happened during the day.' This type of structure is effective here, as it enables the reader to understand why Rosabel feels uncomfortable and unhappy as she journeys home on the bus.

The first half of the text is descriptive as it describes Rosabel's thoughts; this is contrasted with the flashback where the writer makes use of dialogue to show Rosabel's encounter with the red-haired girl and Harry. This helps to establish the characters and to illustrate Rosabel's politeness towards the customer which masks her real feelings.

Although the predominant structural feature is the flashback there is also a cyclical nature to the source as it begins with a reference to the food Rosabel has consumed and the fact that she is still hungry. Rosabel's longing for a good dinner at the start is contrasted with the girl's casual reference to going to lunch with Harry at the end. The contrasting means of transport are also referenced as the red-haired girl's private carriage contrasts with Rosabel's unpleasant journey on public transport. These references to food and transport allow the reader to clearly understand the very different social backgrounds of the two young women.

By the end we also gain an insight to why Rosabel apparently wasted money buying a bunch of violets, rather than the more essential food, at the beginning of the source. It would appear that her purchase was some sort of psychological compensation for the hat that suited her, but she would never be able to afford. The violets were equally indulgent but within her means. Although Rosabel is poor the structure makes it clear to the reader that she aspires to a more glamorous life.

4. Evaluation.

Focus this part of your answer on the second part of
the source, from line 19 to the end. A student said,
'This part of the story, set in the hat shop, shows that
the red-haired girl has many advantages in life, and I
think Rosabel is right to be angry.' To what extent do
you agree?

In your response, you could:

• consider your own impressions of the red-haired girl

• evaluate how the writer conveys Rosabel's reactions
to the red-haired girl

• support your response with references to the text.
(20 marks)

In this evaluation task candidates are invited to
consider whether Rosabel was right to be angry. In
order to access the higher levels on this, the highest
value question on the English Language examination, it
is essential you address the writer's methods; in other
words not just **what** happens, but **how** the writer
presents the events.

This is a subtle piece of writing which allows for
different interpretations and evaluations; however it is
irrelevant whether you believe Rosabel was right to be
angry or not; students are rewarded for how effectively
they **evaluate** the writer's methods.

An overall impression or conclusion could be that
Rosabel isn't right to be angry because the red-haired
girl was perfectly polite to her, but it is understandable,
as the girl appeared to be so privileged whilst Rosabel

was disadvantaged. We will now examine **how** Katherine Mansfield conveys the situation.

We have already been made aware that Rosabel has been irritated by earlier customers before the red-haired girl arrives. The description of the girl, 'beautiful red hair and white skin and eyes the colour of that green ribbon shop with gold they had got from Paris last week' is from Rosabel's viewpoint and suggests she is immediately jealous of the girl's attractive appearance. 'Rosabel had seen her carriage at the door' indicates the girl is privileged to have her own carriage, and this contrasts with Rosabel's subsequent unpleasant bus journey described at the beginning of the source.

The dialogue begins with the girl asking Harry, 'what is it exactly that I want?' as Rosabel attends to her. This could suggest that she has come into the shop casually without any particular purchase in mind, but she has the means to buy anything that takes her fancy.

After Harry describes in detail the kind of hat she should have, 'she glanced at Rosabel laughingly.' The adverb is a significant detail, as it can be interpreted in different ways. On a basic level it could simply show that the girl is happy, however Rosabel may interpret it as the girl is mocking her. A third interpretation could be that the girl, whilst having no thought of mocking Rosabel and simply demonstrating her happiness, is rather thoughtless and shows no understanding of the life and feelings of a humble shop assistant. However, it could also be acknowledged that the girl, like Rosabel, is merely a product of her upbringing and simply has no conception of how those less privileged are compelled to live. This lack of insight would be very much a feature of the time the narrative takes place for many higher-class younger people, as they wouldn't have access to modern media revealing to them a world outside their own. Although there are no right and wrong interpretations, the writer can be credited with presenting an effective detail which allows for a variety of interpretations. This is an example of how the source can be positively evaluated.

Mansfield then contrasts the dialogue with a short narrative paragraph detailing how 'they had been very hard to please' and 'Rosabel was almost in despair.' This gives variety to the writing and sustains the reader's interest as it moves events on swiftly.

Dialogue is reintroduced with Rosabel's polite address to the girl. 'Oh, one moment Madam,' she had said, 'I think perhaps I can show you something that will please you better.' The courteous form of address demonstrates the deferential attitude a shop assistant would be expected to show to a customer, whilst the modal auxiliary verb 'perhaps' suggests Rosabel isn't confident that she will be able to please the girl.

The author effectively makes use of sentence structure as Rosabel goes upstairs to get the hat she hopes will please them. 'She had run up, breathlessly, cut the cords, scattered the tissue paper, and yes, there was the very hat - rather large, with a great, curled feather and a black velvet rose, nothing else.' The punctuation in this long sentence effectively enacts Rosabel's tension and breathlessness as she hopes to find a hat which will please the customer.

Harry and the girl are charmed by the hat, and the author then introduces another detail which provokes ambivalent feelings in the reader, as the girl says to Rosabel, 'Let me see how it looks on you.' It could be argued that this is rather tactless as Rosabel isn't really in a position to refuse. When Rosabel tries the hat on and turns to face them, the girl smiles again and says, 'It suits you beautifully.' It seems to be this that makes

Rosabel angry, although she cannot show her anger. It is perfectly understandable why Rosabel feels this way, as not only could she never afford the hat, but the girl has effectively dehumanised her by treating her as if she is a mannequin rather than a human being with feelings. When the girl smiles at her Rosabel could also feel that she is mocking her again and suggesting that she will never be able to afford the hat. To compound Rosabel's knowledge that she would never own the hat the girl had already cried, 'I must have that!' The modal auxiliary and exclamation mark emphasise that the hat will never be accessible to Rosabel. The girl was perhaps thoughtless, as although it was Rosabel's job to courteously attend to her and serve her, it wasn't her role to be treated as a model.

The paragraph, 'A sudden, ridiculous feeling of anger had seized Rosabel. She longed to throw the lovely perishable thing in the girl's face and bent over the hat, flushing' clearly reveals her feelings. The adjective 'ridiculous' shows that Rosabel is aware her anger is stupid and futile, and her embarrassment suggested as she flushes bending over the hat trying to hide her annoyance and mortification. She politely says to the girl, 'It's exquisitely finished off inside Madam,' to cover her embarrassment.

'The girl swept out to her carriage, and left Harry to pay and bring the box with him,' effectively demonstrates how the girl's life is different to Rosabel's. She can buy an expensive item and leave someone else to pay for it and carry it for her, whilst the verb 'swept' suggests she moves proudly and even majestically like a princess or a queen. The writer effectively ends the passage when the girl casually suggests she will wear the hat for lunch with Harry, as this reminds the reader that Rosabel was hungry at the beginning of the narrative.

Through effective details Katherine Mansfield successfully presents a situation which can be interpreted in different ways by readers. It is possible to understand Rosabel's feelings and sympathise with her situation whilst believing she wasn't right to be angry with the girl, as the red-haired girl had been completely polite towards her throughout the encounter. On the other hand, it could be asserted that although she remained courteous, the girl has been rather tactless and shown a lack of awareness of Rosabel's feelings when she asked her to try the hat on.

The following non-fiction source is taken from a Wjec-Eduquas non-fiction specimen paper.

It has been chosen because the writer employs language techniques already discussed, so once again we can see them in action. As you read it try to identify the language techniques the writer uses to create a light-hearted, self-mocking tone, particularly in the first half of the source. An annotated version follows.

Non-Fiction

Reinventing the Wheel.

Charles Starmer-Smith rediscovers a lost love.

My own conversion to cycling has come late. I remember childhood holidays in France where I would pedal among the villages in search of bread and adventure, revelling in the freedom of pedal power as I sped past vineyards, forests and fields, imagining I was one of the Tour de France greats.

Then came adolescence and girls and guitars and cars and the limitations of a bike, rather than its freedoms, became all too apparent. It couldn't play Pearl Jam on the stereo, with the roof down and a pretty girl in the passenger seat, like my battered silver Mini.

However, there is nothing like purchasing new gear to give you an inflated sense of your sporting prowess. Only a week ago, tackling the gentle contours of Richmond Park, I was puffing like a man on an epic ascent of some legendary Alpine peak. Now, dressed in the outfit I spent a small fortune on this morning, I stride down the stairs with new purpose, ready to join the British Lycra Brotherhood. I feel streamlined and ready for anything the Alps of Surrey can throw at me.

'I want a divorce.' My wife's words stop me in my tracks. She looks both amused and horrified as I put on my helmet and fluorescent bib. 'You look like a Village People tribute act.' Deflated, I hurry past the mirror and wheel my bike out into the winter drizzle for the short journey to the North Downs.

A wave of smugness washes over me as I weave easily through the noisy commuters and choking traffic which stall everyone else's progress. One right turn towards Box Hill and suddenly…silence…

The North Downs Way, which runs from Hampshire through Surrey, awaits. The first rays of sun streak across the chalk hillside, but there's still a chill in the air. I zip up my jersey, looking enviously at the thick coats of the sheep. But I soon forget the cold. With the wind at my back I hear the hum of the tyres and the whirr of the chain. Below me a patchwork of green fields. No deadlines. No delays… For these precious moments I care for little but the verdant hills and plunging valleys - and the panoramic views my efforts have earned.

The British Lycra Brotherhood - for whom mornings, evenings, weekends and holidays are all about pedal power and for whom travel is not just about the destination but the journey there - can welcome its latest recruit. My love of cycling has come full circle.

But how has it come to this? The rise of cycling in Britain has been well documented. A string of champions on the track, from Chris Hoy to Victoria Pendleton, and now on the road, with the new Sky team led by Bradley Wiggins, have done much to inspire a generation of Britons onto their bikes.

Aided by an overpriced and overcrowded transport system and savings from the cycle to work initiative, the bicycle is now seen as an answer to rising carbon emissions. But it is the escapism it gives that is the real draw. You don't need to emulate the endless wave of intrepid cyclists crossing the Americas or circumnavigating the globe to be part of this revolution.

The landscape of Britain is perfect for cycling. Across every hill and valley, country lane and woodland track, the national cycle network covers a mind-boggling 10,000 miles, and we are clocking more than 1,000,000 journeys on these routes each day.

Annotated Source.

My own conversion to cycling has come late. I remember childhood holidays in France - effective beginning using personal experience - where I would pedal among the villages in search of bread and adventure, revelling in the freedom of pedal power as I sped past vineyards, forests and fields, - Triplet quickly conveys the scenery. 'Forests and fields' juxtaposed for alliterative effect - imagining I was one of the Tour de France greats.

Then came adolescence and girls and guitars and cars. - Triplet. 'Girls and guitars' juxtaposed for alliterative effect. 'And' repeated for emphasis, more effective here than using a comma. Cycling was no longer cool - very easy for a modern reader to miss this is still non-standard use of the word 'cool' (fashionable / trendy) and contributes towards the informal, light-hearted, self-deprecating tone - and the limitations of a bike, rather than its freedoms, became all too apparent. It couldn't play Pearl Jam on the stereo, - specific example, rather than using the general word 'music' and helps to establish the writer's character and age group - with the roof down and a pretty girl in the passenger seat, like my battered silver Mini.

However, there is nothing like purchasing new gear to give you an inflated sense of your sporting prowess. Only a week ago, tackling the gentle contours of Richmond Park, I was puffing like a man on an epic ascent of some legendary Alpine peak. - Simile helps the reader to visualise him. Much more effective than simply writing 'I was out of breath.' - Now, dressed in the outfit I spent a small fortune on this morning, I stride - verb chosen for effect, shows his confidence and sense of purpose - down the stairs with new purpose, ready to join the British Lycra Brotherhood - made up term, enhances the light-hearted tone. I feel streamlined and ready for anything the Alps of Surrey can throw at me. - Irony (there are no Alps of Surrey) and metaphor 'throw at me'. Again contributes towards the humorous tone.

'I want a divorce.' My wife's words stop me in my tracks. - Direct speech placed at the beginning of the paragraph for dramatic effect, makes the reader believe for an instant she is serious, much more effective than structuring it, 'My wife said, "I want a divorce" where the impact would be lost. - She looks both amused - suggests she isn't serious - and horrified as I put on my helmet and fluorescent bib. 'You look like a Village People tribute act.' - Very effective cultural reference would allow readers of a certain age to visualise his appearance. Even readers who aren't familiar with the Village People, would understand from the context and 'tribute act' means it is not a flattering reference. Much more effective and humorous rather than merely saying, 'You look stupid.' Deflated, - frontal adjective to emphasise his feelings - I hurry past the mirror and wheel my bike out into the winter drizzle for the short journey to the North Downs.

A wave of smugness washes over me - metaphor effectively showing his feelings of superiority as he goes past the stationary traffic - as I weave easily through the noisy commuters and choking traffic which stall everyone else's progress. One right turn towards Box Hill and suddenly...silence. - Effective use of ellipses to create suspense at the end of the paragraph. Has he had an accident?

The North Downs Way, which runs from Hampshire through Surrey, awaits. The first rays of sun streak across the chalk hillside, but there's still a chill in the air. I zip up my jersey, looking enviously at the thick coats of the sheep. But I soon forget the cold. With the wind at my back I hear the hum of the tyres and the whirr of the chain. Below me a patchwork of green fields. No deadlines. No delays. - Two short sentences suggesting his speed - For these precious moments I care for little but the verdant hills and plunging valleys - and the panoramic views my efforts have earned. - Circular structure used, as his description of the countryside recalls his description of his childhood holidays spent cycling in France in the opening paragraph. This gives a specific example which relates to the main topic of the article - his regaining his love for cycling.

The British Lycra Brotherhood - for whom mornings, evenings, weekends and holidays are all about pedal power and for whom travel is not just about the destination but the journey there - can welcome its latest recruit. My love of cycling has come full circle. - Discourse marker. Positive sentence effectively concludes the personal experience part of the text.

But how has it come to this? - Discourse marker. Question introduces his widening the topic to the modern popularity of cycling in general. - The rise of cycling in Britain has been well documented. A string of champions on the track, from Chris Hoy to Victoria Pendleton, and now on the road, with the new Sky team led by Bradley Wiggins, have done much to inspire a generation of Britons onto their bikes.

Aided by an overpriced and overcrowded transport system and savings from the cycle to work initiative, the bicycle is now seen as an answer to rising carbon emissions. But it is the escapism it gives that is the real draw. You don't need to emulate the endless wave of intrepid cyclists crossing the Americas or circumnavigating the globe to be part of this revolution. Possibly this is hyperbole for humour.

The landscape of Britain is perfect for cycling. Across every hill and valley, country lane and woodland track, - triplet quickly conveys the variety of the national cycle network - the national cycle network covers a mind-boggling 10,000 miles, and we are clocking more than 1,000,000 journeys on these routes each day. Statistics give authority.

Note: the last three paragraphs become more formal as the writer opens the article out to discuss the popularity of cycling in general. He utilises the classic structure of beginning an article with personal experience (and a light-hearted, self-deprecating tone), before discussing the subject in wider detail, bringing in statistics. Beginning with the personal or specific (and humorous wherever possible and suitable for purpose and audience) then opening out to a wider discussion, utilising facts and figures to give authority, is usually the most effective type of structure to immediately engage readers.

Finally, in the response to reading chapter the following two sources are taken from an OCR fiction specimen paper. They have been chosen as they are both interesting sources which allow for rewarding analysis.

The first is a single paragraph of an extract from Clive James autobiography. It has been selected for the following language and structure analysis task.

Look again at lines 12 - 21.

How does Clive James use language and structure to make his description of Mr Ryan's lesson entertaining?

You should use relevant subject terminology to support your answer.
(6 marks)

This is an abridged extract from Clive James's autobiography 'Unreliable Memoirs' published in 1980. Here he describes his experiences of life at school.

I was coping with physics and chemistry well enough while Mr Ryan was still teaching them. But Mr Ryan was due for retirement, an event which was hastened by an accident in the laboratory. He was showing us how careful you had to be when handling potassium in the presence of water. Certainly you had to be more careful then he was. The school's entire supply of potassium was ignited at once. Wreathed by dense smoke and lit by garish flames, the stunned Mr Ryan looked like an ancient Greek god in receipt of bad news. The smoke enveloped us all. Windows being thrown open, it jetted into what passed for a playground, where it hung around like some sinister leftover from a battle on the Somme. Shocked, scorched and gassed, Mr Ryan was carried away never to return.

Suggested response

Although this is a serious and potentially dangerous incident, the writer uses language and structure to make it entertaining and humorous for the reader. It employs a linear structure where one event chronologically follows another. This is the most appropriate structure to describe such an incident, as it allows the reader to follow events in the order they took place and creates a desire to read on in order to find out what happened next; so we are told, "He was showing us how careful you had to be when handling potassium in the presence of water.' This is immediately followed by, 'Certainly you had to be more careful than he was.' These two sentences juxtaposed with each other indicate to the reader that Mr Ryan hasn't adhered to his own warning, and that something potentially interesting and entertaining is about to follow.

James employs an entertaining sentence to describe Mr Ryan's appearance after he had accidently ignited the potassium. 'Wreathed by dense smoke and lit by garish flames, the stunned Mr Ryan looked like an ancient Greek god in receipt of bad news.' The verb 'wreathed' at the beginning of the sentence is effective, as it is not only more unusual than 'covered', it has positive connotations, such as adorned or garlanded, which makes its use amusing. The adjectives 'dense' and 'garish' effectively describe the smoke and flames, bringing the scene alive for the reader. The simile which follows is also entertaining as it is highly unusual. It isn't certain what James means by this, but perhaps Mr Ryan appears very angry that he has suffered an accident in front of the class by not following his own safety advice. Furthermore, Greek gods had special powers which sometimes they lost as punishment for misdeeds; perhaps the writer is suggesting Mr Ryan has now lost his power or control over both his subject and his students.

After this relatively long sentence James follows it with a short one for variety. 'The smoke enveloped us all,' concisely sums up the situation. The structure of this sentence is more effective than 'we were enveloped by smoke,' as it makes the smoke seem more active. Similarly, 'windows being thrown open' is more effective than 'we opened the windows', as it dramatically conveys the urgency of the situation. The phrase 'what passed for a playground' also adds a touch of humour and sustains the light-hearted tone.

Another entertaining simile is used to personify the smoke, 'where it hung around like some sinister leftover from a battle on the Somme.' This vividly conveys the effects of the smoke, again making it seem active. A triplet describes Mr Ryan, 'Shocked, scorched and gassed,' the alliteration emphasises the effect the explosion had upon him.

The final sentence, 'Mr Ryan was carried away, never to return' is effective as it suggests Mr Ryan was incapacitated, however the writer has omitted to say he was carried away to hospital', as this allows him to create an ambivalent ending, and despite the potential seriousness of the teacher's injuries, maintain the entertaining and light-hearted tone.

The companion text on this OCR specimen fiction paper is from the novel *The Prime of Miss Jean Brodie* by Muriel Spark.

Fiction

This is an abridged extract from the novel 'The Prime of Miss Jean Brodie' by Muriel Spark, published in 1961.

Miss Brodie is a teacher at a girls' school. Miss Mackay is the headmistress. The extract takes place at the beginning of the school year. Miss Brodie has recently returned from a holiday in Italy.

'Good morning, sit down, girls,' said the headmistress who had entered in a hurry leaving the door wide open.

Miss Brodie passed behind her with her head up, up, and shut the door with the utmost meaning.

'I have only just looked in,' said Miss Mackay, 'and I have to be off. Well, girls, this is the first day of the new session. Are we downhearted? No. You girls must work hard this year at every subject and pass your qualifying examination with flying colours. Next year you will be in the Senior school, remember. I hope you've all had a nice summer holiday, you all look nice and brown. I hope in due course of time to read your essays on how you spend them.

When she had gone Miss Brodie looked hard at the door for a long time. A girl, call Judith, giggled. Miss Brodie said to Judith, 'That will do.' She turned to the blackboard and rubbed out with a duster the long division sum she always kept on the blackboard in case of intrusions from outside during any arithmetic periods when Miss Brodie should happen not to be teaching arithmetic. When she had done this she turned back to the class and said, are we downhearted no, are we downhearted no. I shall be able to tell you a great deal this term. As you know, I don't believe in talking down to children, you are capable of grasping more than is generally appreciated by your elders. Examination or no qualifying examination, you will have the benefit of my experiences in Italy. In Rome I saw the Coliseum where gladiators died and the slaves were thrown to the Lions. A vulgar American remarked to me, "It looks like a mighty fine quarry." They talk nasally. Mary, what does to talk nasally mean?'

Mary did not know.

'Stupid as ever,' said Miss Brodie. 'Eunice?'

'Through your nose,' said Eunice

'Answer in complete sentences please,' said Miss Brodie. 'This year I think you must all start answering in complete sentences, I must try to remember this rule. Your correct answer is, "To talk nasally means to talk through one's nose". The American said, "It looks like a mighty fine quarry." Ah, it was there the gladiators fought. "Hail Caesar!' they cried. "These about to die salute thee!"

Miss Brodie stood in her brown dress like a gladiator with raised arm and eyes flashing like a sword. 'Hail Caesar!' she cried again, turning radiantly to the window light as if Caesar sat there. Who opened the window?' said Miss Brodie dropping her arm.

Nobody answered.

'Whoever has opened the window has opened it too wide,' said Miss Brodie. 'Six inches is perfectly adequate. More is vulgar. One should have an innate sense of these things. We ought to be doing history at the moment according to the timetable. Get out your history books and prop them up in your hands. I shall tell you a little more about Italy.

Keep your books propped up in case we have any further intruders.' She looked disapprovingly towards the door and lifted her fine dark Roman head with dignity.

'Next year,' she said, 'you will have the specialists to teach you history and mathematics and languages, a teacher for this and a teacher for that. But in this your last year with me you will receive the fruits of my prime. They will remain with you all your days. First, however, I must mark the register for today before we forget. There are two new girls. Stand up the two new girls.'

They stood up with wide eyes while Miss Brodie sat down at a desk.

'You will get used to our ways.'

This source has been chosen for the following task.

Look again at lines 1 - 23 (up to where she asks Mary the question).

Explore how the writer presents Miss Brodie's attitude towards Miss Mackay, the headmistress.

Support your ideas by referring to the language and structure of this section, using relevant subject terminology.　　　　　　(12 marks)

<u>Suggested response</u>

This is a rewarding source, because in the extract Muriel Spark subtly implies Miss Brodie's attitude towards Miss Mackay without stating it. It is a classic example of the writer **showing** through small details rather than **telling**, which is more effective as readers enjoy working out narrative features, such as relationships between characters, rather than merely being told. We will now explore **how** the author does this.

The use of the classroom door is important. The Headmistress enters and leaves the door wide open. Miss Brodie passes behind her and shuts the door 'with the utmost meaning.' It is obvious from this phrase that Miss Brodie isn't happy that Miss Mackay has left the door open. Her attitude towards the headmistress is thereby immediately suggested. The door is referred to again, as after Miss Mackay leaves, 'Miss Brodie looked hard at the door for a long time.' It is as though she is hoping the Headmistress will not return again soon. Spark then inserts a humorous effective detail as, 'A girl, called Judith, giggled.' It is almost as if Judith knows what Miss Brodie is thinking, thereby confirming it for the reader. Rather than saying anything disparaging about the Headmistress Miss Brodie admonishes Judith for giggling. This is a subtler touch from the author as it suggests Miss Brodie is attempting to keep classroom discipline, whilst at the same time allowing the girls to witness her contempt for Miss Mackay.

Miss Brodie's attitude towards the Headmistress is confirmed as she echoes the Headmistresses words, 'Are we downhearted, no.' Although these are the same words the Headmistress used, Miss Brodie's echoing of them is subtly different. Firstly, she repeats the phrase, whereas Miss Mackay said it once, and unlike the

Headmistress, Miss Brodie doesn't phrase it as a question, denoted by the absence of the question mark. By turning the Headmistress's question into a statement it would appear Miss Brodie is implying the girls should not be downhearted, not because they should be confident of rising to the academic challenge, but because they will receive the 'fruits of her prime'. It is as if by repeating Miss Mackay's phrase she is mocking the Headmistress. Her contempt for Miss Mackay is confirmed when she says to the class, 'As you know, I don't believe in talking down to children, you are capable of grasping more than is generally appreciated by your elders.' Here Miss Brodie seems to be implying that the Headmistress has just 'talked down' to them.

The Headmistress had stressed the importance of the qualifying examination in her little pep talk. 'You girls must work hard this year at every subject and pass your qualifying examination with flying colours.' Miss Brodie then dismisses the examination, instead suggesting that listening to her life experiences will be more beneficial to the girls. 'Examination or no qualifying examination, you will have the benefit of my experiences in Italy.'

Without having Miss Brodie say anything directly derogatory about Miss Mackay, Muriel Spark has unequivocally made clear to the reader Miss Brodie's contemptuous and dismissive attitude towards the Headmistress through the symbolism of the door and Miss Brodie's repeating of Miss Mackay's words. The detail of Judith giggling clearly shows the girls are also aware of Miss Brodie's attitude towards the Headmistress. The writing is highly effective as it shows readers Miss Brodie's attitude rather than telling them.

Four

Writing Tasks

The writing task on Paper One of the First AQA Specimen Paper.

(Note: all examination boards produce at least one specimen paper for teachers and students to use as practice before a new examination goes live. AQA produced three specimen papers).

AQA (and some of the other boards) now give a photograph as stimuli for the writing task on Paper One (fiction). There is a choice of either a descriptive task or a story. Not for many years, predating the author's teaching experience, has a creative writing task been set on an examination paper; creative writing was previously confined to coursework and subsequently controlled assessments, thereby allowing students at least several hours (and in the time of coursework sometimes weeks) to work on a story; as this time is now limited to 45 minutes, the task has become much more demanding. To think up a coherent story and complete it satisfactorily after being confronted with a previously unfamiliar image in just 45 minutes is extremely challenging. Although some students with strong imaginative capabilities might wish to accept the challenge of the story, it is strongly advised that most candidates should choose the descriptive piece. There is the strong visual focus of the photograph to assist, and students making this choice do not have the challenge of shaping a coherent narrative in such a limited time.

With this advice in mind, the response to this paper is confined to an example and analysis of the descriptive task only.

There follows the photograph from the first AQA specimen paper. Subsequent ones from AQA and other boards have featured amongst others: a beach scene, a funfair, a rollercoaster, a lake shore with a rear shot of a person, a park at night, a cave, passengers travelling on a bus and a close-up photograph of an elderly man. The photograph could therefore feature either a landscape or people or both.

At this point I feel it necessary to make an important digression regarding some personal experiences of students losing significant marks owing to their failure to address the tasks.

I had a retake student who, when confronted with the photograph of the elderly man in the examination he had recently taken, had written about the problems old people can face in society, rather than writing a description or story inspired by the photograph. The student had in effect produced a discursive non-fiction response more suited to Paper Two. This was one of the reasons he wasn't successful in his initial examination. Similarly, recently, on a Literature paper when responding to the question, 'How far does J.B. Priestly present Mrs Birling as an unlikeable character in *An Inspector Calls?*', very many students wrote about Mr Birling, thereby losing marks for not addressing the task asked of them. This failing to respond to tasks isn't a recent phenomenon; many years ago I had a very able class, half of whom analysed a text in a mock examination when they should have simply summarised. Therefore, although they made some excellent comments about language effects, they could not be credited on this question at all for their insight, as they had not done what they were asked to do, which was to simply summarise the text.

A fundamental piece of advice on any examination paper in any subject is read the question carefully and do what it asks you to do. For example, if it asks you to summarise don't analyse or vice-versa, and if it asks you to produce a piece of fiction do not write a non-fiction response. This may seem obvious advice, but many students carelessly throw marks away by not addressing tasks properly.

After that important digression, back to the imaginative / descriptive writing task. Regardless of the image, remember the photograph is merely there to stimulate the imagination and does not have to be slavishly followed. You will be assessed on the quality of your writing rather than how closely you have described the photograph.

For example, a weak opening for a description of the following photograph would be something like, 'There is a train travelling past some huge waves...'

Similarly, a poor beginning to a description of the second specimen paper beach scene would be, 'There are lots of people on the beach. Children are playing and some adults are sunbathing.' This is too literal, unimaginative and doesn't have anywhere to go. Despite this, it is an approach many students take.

Ensure your response is an **imaginative** one which makes use of interesting adjectives and figurative language and isn't merely limited to a literal description.

Section B: Writing

You are advised to spend about 45 minutes on this section.
Write in full sentences.
You are reminded of the need to plan your answer.
You should leave enough time to check your work at the end.

| 0 | 5 | You are going to enter a creative writing competition.

Your entry will be judged by a panel of people of your own age.

Either: Write a description suggested by this picture:

Or: Write the opening part of a story about a place that is severely affected by the weather.

(24 marks for content and organisation
16 marks for technical accuracy)
[40 marks]

The author's own response, completed within the allocated time, is given below. The reader is advised to read the response carefully, noting the techniques used. The response is reproduced subsequently with analytical annotation to illustrate the language techniques employed.

Sample response to Writing Task One AQA Specimen Paper One. (Paper One Fiction).

Mountainous waves crashing against the glass, wild water insistently hammering at the windows, a howling gale shaking and rocking the trembling train like a pack of slavering hounds ferociously fighting over a single bone. Negotiating the fearsome tempest was like travelling through a gigantic car wash from which we may not emerge alive. Many passengers simply shut their eyes and prayed to every God they believed in and some they had just invented, but I was resolutely drawn to stare through the windows, spellbound by nature's spectacular performance. As far as I was concerned, she was the only God who had the power to take us or to spare us.

Far below the raging, tumultuous sea was instant oblivion for anyone foolish enough to challenge it. Small boats promptly shredded to plywood and even the strongest vessels would be quickly sucked under and disappear forever, digested by the hungry ocean's insatiable appetite.

Another huge surge, almost tossing the train off its tracks like a Scalectrix car at the mercy of a mischievous child. Someone screamed, others joined in. Soon the carriage was a shrieking chorus of terrified humanity, every one of them realising their impotent vulnerability in the face of overwhelming force. We can fly to the moon, live a hundred years and communicate across the world in a minute, but we can never tame ever changeable nature, the most unfathomable of all phenomena. When she is in this mood we are nothing more than her playthings, with which to do as she wishes, who can only hope she will relent once she has made a statement - a statement that, despite Man's advances and achievements, it is Mother Nature alone who really commands our earth.

Eventually, the stomach-churning storm began to slowly subside, and the train pulled gratefully into the station. The terrifying tempest had finally abated as the sobbing travellers disembarked, stepping onto the platform with sweet relief, the terminus of the journey they will never forget. One which could quite easily, had Mother Nature so wished, have been their final destination.

Annotated response to writing task one (Fiction).

Mountainous waves crashing against the glass, wild water insistently hammering at the windows, a howling gale shaking and rocking the trembling train - active present progressive verbs to create a sense of on-going action - like a pack of slavering hounds ferociously fighting - simile and alliteration to suggest the violence of the storm - over a single bone. Negotiating the fearsome tempest - synonym for storm for lexical variety - was like travelling through a gigantic car wash from which we may not emerge alive - simile reflecting the ordeal. Many passengers simply shut their eyes and prayed to every God they believed in and some they had just invented, - shows the passengers desperation and a touch of dark humour - but I was resolutely drawn to stare through the windows, spellbound by nature's spectacular performance. - Alliteration for rhythmic effect. - As far as I was concerned, she was the only God who had the power to take us or to spare us.

Far below the raging, tumultuous sea was instant oblivion - this is preferable to 'instant death' as it is rhythmically better, and 'oblivion' suggests they have disappeared - for anyone foolish enough to challenge it. Small boats promptly shredded - deliberate omission of the auxiliary verb 'were shredded' tightens the rhythm - to plywood and even the strongest vessels - synonym for boats for lexical variety - would be quickly sucked under and disappear forever, digested by the hungry ocean's insatiable appetite - metaphor personifying the ocean, making it seem deliberately cruel.

Another huge surge, almost tossing - verb chosen deliberately to suggest the casual nature of the action - the train off its tracks like a Scalectrix car - simile to illustrate the action - at the mercy of a mischievous child - alliteration for the rhythm, sounds better than 'a naughty child'. Someone screamed, others joined in. Short sentence for grammatical variety and to show the tension. Soon the carriage was a shrieking chorus of terrified humanity, every one of them realising their impotent vulnerability in the face of overwhelming force. We can fly to the moon, live a hundred years and communicate across the world in a minute, but we can never tame ever changeable nature, - assonance for rhythmic effect - the most unfathomable of all phenomena. -Triplet illustrating Mankind's technical achievements. - When she is in this mood, we are nothing more than her playthings, with which to do as she wishes, who can only hope she will relent once she has made a statement - a statement that, despite Man's advances and achievements, - embedded subordinate clause links back to the triplet giving examples - it is Mother Nature alone who really commands our earth.

Eventually, the stomach-churning storm began to slowly subside, - alliteration for rhythmic effect - and the train pulled gratefully - metaphor concisely suggesting the feelings of the passengers - into the station. The terrifying tempest - alliteration for rhythmic effect - had finally abated as the sobbing travellers disembarked, - lexis chosen for conciseness and rhythm, more sophisticated than saying 'as they got off' - stepping onto the platform with sweet relief, - assonance for rhythmic effect - the terminus of the journey - assonance for rhythmic effect - they will never forget. One which could quite easily, had Mother Nature so wished, - embedded subordinate clause for emphasis and sophistication - have been their final destination.

Sometimes it may be difficult to know how to conclude a descriptive piece, as unlike a narrative, there may not be an obvious beginning, middle and end. As it was a photograph of a train travelling this particular option lent itself to an obvious ending, or choice of endings: either the train could arrive safely at its destination or come to grief in the storm. As I wanted a positive ending I opted for the former. If the photograph is static the ending might not be so obvious.

The writing task on Paper Two of the First AQA Specimen Paper.

The writing task on Paper 2 of the AQA language examination is a non-fiction piece requiring candidates to write to argue and persuade. It usually takes the form of a statement and invites candidates to write their views on this statement. Unlike the fiction writing task on Paper 1, AQA do not offer a choice on Paper 2, and only one task is set. However, the subject matter will always be accessible to young people. For example: sport, animal welfare, travel, healthy lifestyles, the environment, relationships with parents or friends, modern technology, or education tend to be common topics.

All examination boards have a similar task on their English language papers, and some may give a choice of writing tasks. There may also be an occasional variation where candidates might be asked to write a transactional piece (a piece of writing designed to get something done) e.g. apply for a job or a course, however writing to argue and persuade is the predominant form of non-fiction writing required by examination boards.

There follows the task set on the first AQA specimen paper. This was a particularly good choice of task, as all students have experience of and views about homework, so it was thoroughly accessible.

'Homework has no value. Some students get it done for them; some don't do it at all. Students should be relaxing in their free time.' Write an article for a broadsheet newspaper in which you explain your point of view on this statement.

(24 marks for content and organisation16 marks for technical accuracy).   [40marks]

The author's own response completed within the allocated time is given below. The reader is advised to read the response carefully, noting the techniques used. The response is reproduced subsequently with analytical annotation to illustrate the language techniques employed.

Sample response to Writing Task Two AQA Specimen Paper One (Paper Two Non -Fiction).

We've all heard the improbable explanations: 'I spilt my dinner on it', 'I was staying at my 'real' dad's at the weekend and I forgot it', or most renowned of all, 'My dog ate it'; just some of the numerous excuses school pupils give for not doing their homework. Indeed, some students don't even bother to cobble up an excuse and just truthfully blurt out, 'I couldn't be bothered.' And who can blame them? After six hours in school who among us would want to spend their evenings suffering further tortuous mathematics, an extra English assignment or even more boring history? Who would wish to waste a glorious sunny weekend stuck indoors slogging away on a geography project, or trying to get to grips with a foreign tongue they will never use once they've finally escaped compulsory education? Yet this is what we expect of our children. all adults, whether they be teachers or parents, are conditioned to believe homework is good, whilst the majority of teenagers think it is a wicked scheme cooked up by oldies jealous of their youth to waste those precious years of innocence and freedom.

Why is it then that teachers are obliged to set homework and parents condition to expect it? One of the reasons is surely that it is always existed. Unlike almost anything else in life, childhood, school days and therefore homework, are experiences shared by everyone. I had to do it, and therefore it's only fair that my darling daughter or precious son should do it too. Like fruit and vegetables, homework is seen as a good thing, whilst to spend any spare time on the PlayStation or Xbox is viewed equivalent to scoffing a family sized bar of chocolate or tucking into a mammoth bag of chips.

However much most young people may despise homework, and some teachers resent the efforts they have to make in order to ensure it is completed on time, there is a point to it, indeed several points. The first one has been touched upon in the previous sentence; 'completed on time' suggests that it teaches teenagers the importance of meeting deadlines, something that many of them will have to get used to in the world of work. Instilling a sense of personal responsibility and the ability to work unsupervised on their own initiative are essential qualities and skills needed in adulthood that can be fostered by regular homework. In addition, completing after school tasks has a direct impact on school work, developing and enhancing the study of all subjects. Indeed, on occasions homework can even be a revelation, allowing some children to experience the thrill of discovering something for themselves or the pride of completing a task without any help. It also has a direct impact on examination results, as research has shown that students who regularly do their homework go on to achieve higher grades, with 67% achieving grade C or better in all subjects.

Of course, homework will always be controversial, because as the statement suggests, there can never be a level playing field; some students will always get more support at home than others, whilst some, unfortunately, won't experience the kind of home environment that is conducive to academic work. However, most modern schools are aware of the problems some pupils may face at home - unsupportive parents, Jack in the Box siblings, having to divide their time between multiple households, or simply the lack of a quiet space in which to work - so provide either lunchtime or after school facilities to allow their pupils to complete homework.

For the reasons outlined above therefore, I believe homework is beneficial to teenagers and not just a cruel punishment devised to spoil their adolescent years or to simply keep them off the streets.

Annotated response to writing task two (Non-fiction).

We've all heard the improbable explanations: 'I spilt my dinner on it', - assonance for rhythmic effect - 'I was staying at my 'real' dad's at the weekend and I forgot it', or most renowned of all, 'My dog ate it'; - triplet showing excuses, the most common placed last, emphasised by embedded subordinate clause - just some of the numerous excuses - assonance for rhythmic effect - school pupils give for not doing their homework. Indeed, some students don't even bother to cobble up - verb chosen deliberately to emphasise the random nature of the excuses - an excuse and just truthfully blurt out, - assonance and verb chosen deliberately to emphasise the random nature of the excuses 'I couldn't be bothered.' And who can blame them? After six hours in school who among us would want to spend their evenings suffering - alliteration for rhythmic effect -

further tortuous mathematics, an extra English assignment or even more boring history? - Triplet giving examples. Assonance for rhythmic effect. - Who would wish to waste - alliteration for rhythmic effect - a glorious sunny weekend stuck indoors slogging away - alliteration for rhythmic effect. Verb chosen deliberately to suggest the difficulty and tedium of the work - on a geography project, or trying to get to grips with a foreign tongue - assonance for rhythm, more rhythmic than 'foreign language' - they will never use once they've finally escaped - verb chosen deliberately to suggest the captive nature of - compulsory education? - Rhetorical questions to engage readers. - Yet this is what we expect of our children. All adults, whether they be teachers or parents, - embedded subordinate clause for emphasis and sophistication - are conditioned to believe homework is good, whilst the majority of teenagers think it is a wicked scheme cooked up - verb chosen deliberately to suggest a wicked spell - by oldies - informal lexis to reflect how the young might view older people - jealous of their youth to waste those precious years of innocence and freedom.

Why is it then that teachers are obliged to set homework and parents condition to expect it? - Rhetorical question to make readers think. - One of the reasons is surely that it is always existed. - Rhetorical question answered. - Unlike almost anything else in life, childhood, school days and therefore homework, - triplet - are experiences shared by everyone. I had to do it, and therefore it's only fair that my darling daughter or precious son - more interesting and specific rather than saying 'children' - should do it too. Like fruit and vegetables, homework is seen as a good thing, whilst to spend any spare time on the PlayStation or X box is viewed equivalent to scoffing - verb chosen deliberately to emphasise greed - a family sized bar of chocolate or tucking - verb deliberately chosen to suggest enjoyment

- into a mammoth - adjectives chosen to suggest size - bag of chips. Similes used to contrast 'good' and 'bad' activities and to make the piece entertaining.
However much most young people may despise homework, and some teachers resent the efforts they have to make in order to ensure it is completed on time, - embedded subordinate clause suggesting teachers also might not like having to set homework - there is a point to it, indeed several points. The first one has been touched upon in the previous sentence; - anaphoric reference to link points - 'completed on time' suggests that it teaches teenagers - alliteration - the importance of meeting deadlines, something that many of them will have to get used to in the world of work. Instilling a sense of personal responsibility and the ability to work unsupervised on their own initiative are essential qualities and skills needed in adulthood that can be fostered by regular homework. In addition, - discourse marker to link points - completing after school tasks has a direct impact on school work, developing and enhancing the study of all subjects. Indeed, on occasions homework can even be a revelation, allowing some children to experience the thrill of discovering something for themselves or the pride of completing a task without any help. It also has a direct impact on examination results as research has shown that students who regularly do their homework go on to achieve higher grades, with 67% achieving grade C or better in all subjects. Statistic to give authority.
Of course, homework will always be controversial, because as the statement suggests, - reference back to the statement given in the task - there can never be a level playing field; - metaphor - some students will always receive more support at home than others, whilst some, unfortunately, won't experience the kind of home environment that is conducive to academic work. However, most modern schools are aware of the

problem some pupils may face at home - unsupportive parents, Jack in the Box siblings, - metaphor helps reader to imagine the lively behaviour of the siblings - having to divide their time between multiple households, or simply the lack of a quiet space in which to work - triplet listing possible problems - so provide either lunchtime or after school facilities to allow their pupils to complete homework. Note, the language of the previous two paragraphs was deliberately more formal than that of the opening two, as having drawn the reader in with entertaining non-standard language it becomes more appropriate to adopt a formal tone to discuss the positive reasons for homework.
For the reasons outlined above therefore, I believe homework is beneficial to teenagers and not just a cruel punishment devised to spoil their adolescent years or to simply keep them off the streets. Logical conclusion.

Another way of opening this response, instead of with the excuses, could be to relate some personal experience such as an anecdote about a specific piece of homework that was especially memorable to you in some way, either positively or negatively. Or perhaps an example of each.

 For example, I could have used a memory of an especially difficult Mathematics homework I was set during my first year at secondary school. Although my memory of it is now very hazy, I vaguely recall struggling horribly with it, and asking my father (who was good at Maths) for help. He too found it difficult; we struggled for what seemed an age, and there were tears and tantrums from yours truly. Although I can't recall the outcome, I do remember it coloured my attitude to Mathematic specifically and homework generally for the rest of my schooldays. From these vague memories I would have been able to embellish events and to construct an alternative personal and humorous opening to the response.

Although on AQA Paper One the writing task usually offers a choice of either writing a descriptive piece inspired by the photograph or a story, on the third specimen paper, rather than a descriptive task, the choice was between two narrative ideas, therefore the recommendation to choose the descriptive option would not have been possible.

The first option was: 'Write a story set on a dark night as suggested by this picture.'

This task was therefore based on the following photograph.

The second choice was, 'Write a story about a game that goes badly wrong.'

Both choices have the word 'story' in the task, and they do overlap to some extent, and, although it is unlikely that a descriptive option won't always be offered in the future, the author has written a response which combines the narrative choices, although ultimately it is a response to the first option inspired by the photograph.

The author's own response completed within the allocated time is given below. The reader is advised to read the response carefully, noting the techniques used. The response is reproduced subsequently with analytical annotation to illustrate the language techniques employed.

The writing task on Paper One of the Third AQA Specimen Paper.

11

Section B: Writing

You are advised to spend about 45 minutes on this section.
Write in full sentences.
You are reminded of the need to plan your answer.
You should leave enough time to check your work at the end.

| 0 | 5 | You have been invited to produce a piece of creative writing about how children play imaginatively.

Either: Write a story set on a dark night as suggested by this picture:

Or: Write a story about a game that goes badly wrong.

(24 marks for content and organisation
16 marks for technical accuracy)
[40 marks]

_____

_____

_____

_____

_____

_____

Typesetter code

Turn over ▶

<u>Sample response to Writing Task One. Specimen</u>
<u>Paper Three (Paper One Fiction).</u>

<u>The Challenge</u>

I have always been one to accept a challenge, so when my friend, Ellie, the unacknowledged leader of our little gang, dared one of us to spend the entire night alone in the park, inevitably I was the one to take on the dare. Everyone else hesitated, plainly fearful to face the risk, but I knew my acceptance of the challenge would elevate me to the number one position - even above Ellie - in our friendship circle. Everyone admires a daredevil, someone who does something others dare not, and I would be the one who would spend the night alone once the park gates were locked, whilst my friends were all tucked up safe and warm in their beds.

All six of us were sitting around in the park that fateful afternoon, but as the gloom gathered and the autumn darkness descended the other girls left before the gates closed at five o clock. I concealed myself behind some bushes as the parkkeeper went upon his rounds, ensuring all was well, before he locked the gates and disappeared for the evening.

I was now alone, suddenly wondering just what I had let myself in for. Rather than a mere fifteen hours away when the gates opened again at eight o clock next morning, it now seemed I had invited a life sentence and escape would be impossible.

I lay down on one of the park benches and made myself as comfortable as I could. Ellie had specified rules for the challenge, precluding any form of comfort or equipment. Basically, I wasn't allowed anything, apart from the clothes I wore. Therefore, I had neither food nor drink to sustain me, nor even a blanket for warmth. Boredom, hunger and cold would be triple challenges, challenges I had anticipated and been prepared for. What I hadn't prepared for was the fourth challenge - fear.

My plan had been to try to go to sleep as soon as I could, hoping the time would pass that way and before I knew it dawn would break, banishing the darkness and heralding the end of my ordeal. However it wasn't to be, as comforting sleep stubbornly stayed away, cold air began to bite, sinking its rapacious jaws deep into my spine, and my fevered imagination started to weave its disturbing spell.

Tree branches swaying in the increasing breeze, like evil demons summoning some wicked spell, shadows dancing, casting unearthly shapes intermittently illuminated by the lamps that lit the path and unseen creatures scurrying in the bushes were malevolent meddlers keeping me from sleep. These, and other indescribable sensations, started to intrude upon my consciousness as fear tightened its unyielding grip and I cursed my reckless acceptance of this challenge.

Then the first lamp suddenly extinguished itself, followed by a second and a third and a fourth, and, within seconds, the path, and the entire park were ruthlessly cast into pitch darkness like the onset of the apocalypse. This was a petrifying development I hadn't anticipated; the lights had given some comfort and now they had been snuffed out like candles signalling the end of life. I longed for a torch to cast its reassuring beam, or a blanket to snuggle beneath as if I were a vulnerable creature hibernating from the lethal winter. However, I had neither; merely my imagination racing relentlessly, dragging me into the infinite pit of interminable nightmares.

Then I saw it, on the next bench but one from mine, a misshapen figure huddled in the shadows. I was sure it hadn't been there before the lights died, but it was certainly there now, the final torment of my terrifying night. What was it? Who was it? A homeless tramp compelled to spend the night in the park? Unlike my stupid, show-off self he probably had no choice, however I had a choice. And I had chosen the wrong one.

I continued to stare at the figure, fearfully hoping it hadn't seen me. For what seemed an age it didn't move. Maybe it was asleep? Or maybe it wasn't a man after all, maybe it was an inanimate bag of trash, but how had it come to be there? I was positive it wasn't there when the lights had illuminated the path. Maybe someone had dumped it there? However, if that was the case then it suggested the equally horrifying prospect that I wasn't alone in this park; someone or something was out there in the darkness.

Suddenly, the screech of some nocturnal creature froze my bones and the hooded figure rose to its feet. It seemed to survey its surroundings before turning towards my direction. It lingered for a sickening second, then began to move, stepping slowly but surely nearer to me. The wind whistled louder, the trees frantically brandished their branches - a mad dance of unforgettable dread - the unseen creatures scurried faster. I cursed Ellie. I condemned myself, as the figure moved ever nearer. Nearer! Suddenly, an ear-splitting crash of thunder! Lightening forked the sky, illuminating the whole area for a few sickening seconds. The figure was immediately before me, instantly upon me. It pulled down its hood, revealing its fiendish features and murderous intent. I screamed! Screamed for my stupidity! Screamed for my safety! Screamed for my life!

Suddenly, I woke. Eventually, I recognised my surroundings, felt the comfort of my bed, the warmth of my duvet, the reassuring tones of my mother who had appeared, disturbed by the sounds of my screams.

The following afternoon, the six of us were again chilling out in the park. Ellie looked at each of us carefully, before challenging, 'Which one of you dare spend the whole night alone in this park?'

With a wicked smile, her gaze remained upon me.

Annotated response to writing task one (Fiction).

The Challenge

I - first person viewpoint, often more effective for thriller / horror genre - have always been one to accept a challenge, - character immediately established - so when my friend, Ellie, the unacknowledged leader of our little gang, dared one of us to spend the entire night alone in the park, inevitably I was the one to take on the dare. Everyone else hesitated, plainly fearful to face the risk, but I knew my acceptance of the challenge would elevate me to the number one position - even above Ellie - in our friendship circle. - Acknowledgement of peer group rivalry and motivation for accepting the challenge. - Everyone admires a daredevil, someone who does something others dare not, and I would be the one who would spend the night alone once the park gates were locked, whilst my friends were all tucked up safe and warm in their beds. - Contrast between the main character's situation and that of her friends.

All six of us were sitting around in the park that fateful afternoon, but as the gloom gathered and the autumn darkness descended - alliteration for rhythmic effect - the other girls left before the gates closed at five o clock. I concealed myself behind some bushes as the parkkeeper went upon his rounds, ensuring all was well, before he locked the gates and disappeared for the evening.

I was now alone, suddenly wondering - assonance for rhythmic effect - just what I had let myself in for. Rather than a mere fifteen hours away when the gates opened again at eight o clock next morning, it now seemed I had invited a life sentence and escape would be impossible.

I lay down on one of the park benches and made myself as comfortable as I could. Ellie had specified rules for the challenge, precluding any form of comfort or equipment. Basically, I wasn't allowed anything, apart from the clothes I wore. Therefore, I had neither food nor drink to sustain me, nor even a blanket for warmth. Boredom, hunger and cold would be triple challenges, challenges I had anticipated and been prepared for. What I hadn't prepared for was the fourth challenge - fear. Dramatic ending to paragraph.

My plan had been to try to go to sleep as soon as I could, hoping the time would pass that way and before I knew it dawn would break, banishing the darkness and heralding the end of my ordeal. - Assonance for rhythmic effect. - However, it wasn't to be, as comforting sleep stubbornly stayed away, - alliteration for rhythmic effect - cold air began to bite, - alliterative metaphor - sinking its rapacious jaws - personification to humanise the cold and emphasise the pain it's causing her - deep into my spine and my fevered imagination started to weave its disturbing spell.-

Metaphor emphasises her imagination is preventing her sleeping and having a disturbing effect upon her.

Tree branches swaying in the increasing breeze, like evil demons summoning some wicked spell, shadows dancing, casting - poetic effect and shift to present progressive verbs to suggest ongoing action, more effective here than past tense - unearthly shapes intermittently illuminated by the lamps that lit the path and unseen creatures - assonance for effect - scurrying - verb chosen to suggest quick, unseen movement - in the bushes were malevolent meddlers - alliteration and metaphor suggesting the creatures are deliberately preventing her sleeping - keeping me from sleep. - Alliteration and assonance for rhythmic effect. - These, and other indescribable sensations, started to intrude upon my consciousness as fear tightened its unyielding grip - personification of fear making it seem a living, concrete danger - and I cursed my reckless acceptance - assonance for rhythmic effect - of this challenge.

Then the first lamp suddenly extinguished itself, - personification of the lamp making its action appear deliberate - followed by a second and a third and a fourth, - repetition of 'and' to emphasise cumulative effect - and within seconds, the path, and the entire park, were ruthlessly cast into pitch darkness - assonance emphasises dramatic nature of onset of darkness - like the onset of the apocalypse. - Simile emphasises the darkness is like the end of the world. - This was a petrifying development I hadn't anticipated; the lights had given some comfort and now they had been snuffed out like candles signalling the end of life. - Simile emphasises the dramatic effect of the darkness. - I longed for a torch to cast its reassuring beam, or a blanket to snuggle beneath as if I were a vulnerable creature hibernating from the lethal winter. - Simile emphasises her vulnerability. - However, I had neither;

merely my imagination racing relentlessly, - alliteration emphasises the speed of her imagination running out of her control - dragging me into the infinite pit of interminable nightmares. - Personification of imagination, making it seem dangerous.

Then I saw it, - dramatic opening to paragraph, neutral pronoun creates mystery - on the next bench but one from mine, a misshapen figure huddled in the shadows. I was sure it hadn't been there before the lights died, - personification humanising the lights and making the situation more atmospheric and threatening - but it was certainly there now, the final torment of my terrifying night. - Alliteration emphasises her terror. - What was it? Who was it? A homeless tramp compelled to spend the night in the park? Questions to stimulate readers' interest and help them relate to her situation. - Unlike my stupid, show-off self he probably had no choice, however I had a choice. And I had chosen the wrong one. - Dramatic ending to paragraph.

I continued to stare at the figure, fearfully hoping it hadn't seen me. For what seemed an age it didn't move. Maybe it was asleep? Or maybe it wasn't a man after all, maybe it was an inanimate bag of trash, - 'trash' chosen for sound, more rhythmic than 'rubbish' - but how had it come to be there? I was positive it wasn't there when the lights had illuminated the path. Maybe someone had dumped it there? - Questions to involve readers. - However, if that was the case then it suggested the equally horrifying prospect that I wasn't alone in this park; someone or something was out there in the darkness. - Dramatic ending to paragraph.

Suddenly, the screech of some nocturnal creature froze my bones - alliteration and assonance to create tension - and the hooded figure rose to its feet. It seemed to survey its surroundings before turning towards my direction. - Alliteration for rhythmic effect. - It lingered for a sickening second then began to move, stepping slowly but surely nearer to me. Alliteration and assonance for rhythmic effect and to emphasise tension. - The wind whistled louder, the trees frantically brandished their branches - a mad dance of unforgettable dread - the unseen creatures scurried faster. - Triplet emphasises her surroundings and rising terror. - I cursed Ellie. I condemned myself, as the figure moved ever nearer. Nearer! - Repetition to emphasise the approaching danger. - Suddenly, an ear-splitting crash of thunder! Lightening forked the sky, illuminating the whole area for a few sickening seconds. - Dramatic weather, appealing to readers' sense of sight and sound. - The figure was immediately before me, instantly upon me. It pulled down its hood, revealing its fiendish features and murderous intent. I screamed! Screamed for my stupidity! Screamed for my safety! Screamed for my life! - Short sentences and repetition for dramatic effect.

Suddenly, I woke. - Note, not 'woke **up**', as the preposition weakens it and ending a sentence on a preposition tends to be clumsy writing. - Eventually, I recognised my surroundings, felt the comfort of my bed, the warmth of my duvet, the reassuring tones of my mother who had appeared, disturbed by the sounds of my screams. -Triplet reflects her slowly gaining consciousness and realising it was a dream. Unnecessary to tell the reader it was a dream. The triplet shows that.

The following afternoon, the six of us were again chilling out in the park. Ellie looked at each of us carefully, before challenging, 'Which one of you dare spend the whole night alone in this park?'

With a wicked smile, her gaze remained upon me. - Ironic ending to give a twist on the cliched 'dream' ending.

'It was all a dream' might be regarded as a somewhat cliched 'cop out' ending, but is one way of bringing a narrative to a conclusion. An alternative ending could have been when the figure pulls its hood down it is revealed to be Ellie playing a trick on the narrator.

A final example of a non-fiction task and response to it is given below.

A very good non-fiction writing task offered a few years ago by an examination board was on the topic of part time jobs, another subject most teenagers would find accessible and hold strong views on. The author's own response completed within the allocated time is given below. The reader is advised to read the response carefully, noting the techniques used. The response is reproduced subsequently with analytical annotation to illustrate the language techniques employed.

'Having a part time job can be an unwanted distraction for teenagers of school age.' Write your views on this statement.

<u>Suggested response.</u>

I will never forget the day I received my first pay packet, not only was I over the moon, I was on my way to Mars too. Although I was only thirteen, I felt really grown up, as if I had unlocked the door to the adult world. While some teenagers take up smoking and drinking to make out they are mature, I took to working. While some of my friends spent their Saturday mornings snoozing in bed I was out grafting. Whilst some youngsters rely on income from their parents, I generated my own. By the time I was sixteen I'd already had a paper round, worked weekends on a market stall and cleaned cars for anyone who would let me near their vehicle with a bucket and a cloth.

I can understand why some people believe teenagers shouldn't take part time jobs, as it might affect their school work and they could become victims of exploitation by unscrupulous employers, however I feel the advantages of working to earn your own money outweigh the drawbacks. Yes, there are bad employers who might seek to take advantage of young people; however, the employment laws regarding using school age children are extremely strict. Teenagers between the ages of thirteen and sixteen are only allowed to work for two hours per day during the week and six hours a day at weekends. Most employers wouldn't risk their businesses by breaking these employment safeguards.

It might be tricky for some kids to balance part time employment with school work; however, I believe this is a learning process and an aspect of growing up. Rather than clashing with school learning commitments, having a part time job can actually enhance your studies in a variety of ways. For example, it helps you to learn to organise your time and to prioritise tasks during the week. Having a job also gives you a sense of responsibility with regard to punctuality, completing tasks and meeting targets, all of which can only be good for your schoolwork. In addition, it increases your confidence.

Furthermore, earning my own income means I don't have to rely on my parents all the time; my iPod and my phone were both purchased with the sweat from my own brow, rather than with theirs, and this makes them proud of me rather than feeling I'm a drain on their purses.

I know not all teenagers enjoy a positive experience when working. For example, a friend told me that when he was working in a kitchen, a frustrated circus performer masquerading as a chef, once hurled a knife at him in a fit of pique. Diced nipples rather than diced carrots were nearly on the menu that day! Fortunately, my friend lived to tell the tale. I can honestly say that nothing like that has ever happened to me, and my experiences of work have always been entirely positive. It would seem that many young people also have constructive experiences of the workplace, as 62% of thirteen to sixteen-year olds claim to have a part time job whilst they are still at school.

In conclusion, I believe that school age children should definitely be allowed to take part time work if they wish to. After all, what could be better than gaining experience, confidence and a sense of responsibility was earning your own money to spend how you want?

Annotated response.

I will never forget the day I received my first pay packet, - personal experience for effective opening - not only was I over the moon, I was on my way to Mars too - a rather cliched metaphor, but with a little twist for variety, suggesting not only was I happy but extremely happy. - Although I was only thirteen, I felt really grown up, as if I had unlocked the door to the adult world - metaphor to give interest to the writing. - While some teenagers take up smoking and drinking to make out they are mature, I took to working. While some of my friends spent their Saturday mornings snoozing - verb chosen deliberately to suggest laziness - in bed I was out grafting - verb chosen deliberately to suggest hard work, also gives lexical variety as 'working' has already been used. - Whilst some youngsters rely on income from their parents, I generated my own. By the time I was sixteen I'd already had a paper round, worked weekends on a market stall and cleaned cars for anyone who would let me near their vehicle with a bucket and a cloth - triplet with a little humour on the last one.

I can understand why some people believe teenagers shouldn't take part time jobs, as it might affect their school work and they could become victims of exploitation by unscrupulous employers, - formal higher-level lexis for variety - however I feel the advantages of working to earn your own money outweigh the drawbacks. Yes, - helps to suggest the writer is speaking directly to the audience - there are bad - basic adjective used for variety after the earlier choice of the similar, but more formal 'unscrupulous' - employers who might seek to take advantage - phrase similar to earlier choice of 'exploitation' used for variety - of young people; however, the employment laws regarding using school age children are extremely strict. Teenagers between the ages of thirteen and sixteen are only allowed to work for two hours per day during the week and six hours a day at weekends. - Statistic to give authority. - Most employers wouldn't risk their businesses by breaking these employment safeguards.

It might be tricky for some kids - non-standard lexical choice for variety - to balance part time employment with school work; however, I believe this is a learning process and an aspect of growing up. Rather than clashing with school learning commitments, - alliteration for emphasis - having a part time job can actually enhance your studies in a variety of ways. For example, it helps you to learn to organise your time and to prioritise tasks during the week. Having a job also gives you a sense of responsibility with regard to punctuality, completing tasks and meeting targets, all of which can only be good for your schoolwork. In addition, it increases your confidence. - Direct address to audience by using second person pronoun and focus on advantages of work.

Furthermore, - discourse marker to link points - earning my own income means I don't have to rely on my parents all the time; my iPod and my phone - specific examples to personalise the text and interest the reader - were both purchased with the sweat from my own brow, - metaphor to make the writing interesting - rather than with theirs, and this makes them proud of me rather than feeling I'm a drain on their purses. - Metaphor to give interest to the writing.

I know not all teenagers enjoy a positive experience when working. - There follows a personal anecdote developed from something a pupil said in class. This is used to personalise and add humour to the piece. His actual words were, 'a chef threw a knife at me.' Note how those seven words have been expanded to over forty. - For example, a friend told me that when he was working in a kitchen, a frustrated circus performer - humorous comparison with someone who might throw knives for a living - masquerading - deliberate choice of verb, more effective than 'pretending' as it is more original and suggests dressing up - as a chef, once hurled - more powerful verb than 'threw' - a knife at him in a fit of pique - more original and humorous than 'anger', as it suggests the chef is having a tantrum. - Diced nipples rather than diced carrots were nearly on the menu that day! - Potentially painful but humorous possible consequences. - Fortunately, my friend lived to tell the tale. - Positive conclusion to anecdote. - I can honestly say that nothing like that has ever happened to me, and my experiences of work have always been entirely positive. - Link to anecdote. - It would seem that many young people also have constructive experiences of the workplace, as 62% of thirteen to sixteen-year olds claim to have a part time job whilst they are still at school. - Statistic to give authority linked to previous anecdote.

In conclusion, - discourse marker to indicate the piece is coming to an end - I believe that school age children should definitely be allowed to take part time work if they wish to. - Personal opinion summing up the issue. - After all, what could be better than gaining experience, confidence and a sense of responsibility than earning your own money to spend how you want? - Concludes with a triplet and a rhetorical question to give an effective ending and leave the audience thinking.

Note, the response follows the classic structure of beginning with personal experience before opening it up to a more generalised discussion of the topic, although a personal anecdote is inserted towards the end to add humour and sustain interest.

Conclusion

This concludes the guide, and if you have made it to the end, I thank you for purchasing it, and hope that it will be of some use in helping you to achieve your English Language GCSE.

To conclude on a positive note it is worth re-emphasising something mentioned earlier. It isn't actually that difficult to achieve a pass grade in English Language (or Literature) provided you demonstrate some understanding and some level of analysis towards texts and your own writing is competent, cohesive and coherent.

Hopefully, this guide has given you some tips, tools and techniques which will enable you not just to pass GCSE English Language, but to pass with flying colours!

Printed in Great Britain
by Amazon